GOLD RUSH

BY
R.K. CHIN

Xulon Elite

Copyright © 2017 by R.K. Chin
2nd edition

Gold Rush
by R.K. Chin

Printed in the United States of America

ISBN 9781498463553

All rights reserved solely by the author. The author guarantees all contents are original and do not infringe upon the legal rights of any other person or work. No part of this book may be reproduced in any form without the permission of the author. The views expressed in this book are not necessarily those of the publisher.

Scripture quotations taken from the Holy Bible, New International Version (NIV). Copyright © 1973, 1978, 1984, 2011 by Biblica, Inc.™. Used by permission. All rights reserved.

www.xulonpress.com

PREFACE

Avid adventurer since the age of sixteen, forty countries explored extensively including six continents in six months, caught the travel bug early which, fortunately, has found no remedy, R.K.C. is a historian intensely curious with anthropology. Having never traveled with any tour group, he just totally immerses with the locals and sees firsthand what makes them tick.

Recording trips by photography, camcorder, GoPro 4K (soon 8K) and drones, he brings the adventure back to those who can't physically go themselves. Upon landing in the States after returning overseas, he grabs his carry-on luggage (a backpack) from the overhead compartment, waits for his turn to exit the plane, walks down the stairs, drops to his knees and kisses the ground.

R.K.C. makes his home wherever he is. In other words, he's always comfortable in his own skin: whatever his surroundings, whether it's at the Waldorf Astoria, Mandarin Hotel in Hong Kong, a lofty South American mountain top, a sweltering African desert oasis, a Southeast Asian land-mined jungle, or even in a RV trailer in the Klondike. "So far, so good," I say.

GOLD RUSH EXPOSED

Exposing myths of not only one of the most popular reality shows of all television history, but the actual progenitor of gold and Alaskan genre.

CONTENTS

Preface..iii
Gold Rush Exposed...iv
Foreword..ix
Dedication...x
Introduction..xi
Thesis...xii
My Gold Rush Thesis...xiii
Unanswered Questions...xiv
1. "The Treasure of the Sierra Madre"....................................1
2. Basics...2
3. Gold Price..5
4. Got Money?...6
5. Giving Good Gifts..14
6. TV Strategy..23
7. Graphic Success...24
8. Auction...25
9. Inviting Kato..27
10. Suckered..30
11. Midnight Walker..30
12. Leaving Sandy Airport..30
13. James' Ghost...33
14. Kato Reincarnated...33
15. Supplanting James...37
16. Girlfriend...37
17. Parole Evidence...38
18. Haines, Alaska...41
19. Provost Marshal...45
20. Bear Hunt..47
21. Jim Dorsey..49
22. Flag Raising..49
23. Forehand Knowledge..50

24.	Losing Control	50
25.	"N" word	50
26.	James' Secret	51
27.	Napoleonic Complex	52
28.	Setting An Example	53
29.	Censorship	55
30.	Bad Mouthing	55
31.	Destination Klondike	56
32.	"Bullitt"	58
33.	Wounded Warriors	63
34.	Front & Center	69
35.	Dave's Expletive	72
36.	Wood Block	73
37.	Another Gold Mine?	73
38.	Soporific	78
39.	Lost Supplies	78
40.	Bigger Heads	80
41.	Sturgeon	80
42.	Finger Pointing	85
43.	Money Over Matter	89
44.	Inner Sanctum	90
45.	Product Placement	91
46.	Hit & Run	91
47.	Confession	97
48.	Old Glory	97
49.	Clint Eastwood Moment	98
50.	Re-shooting Script	101
51.	Stanford	103
52.	Sacrificial Lamb	104
53.	Chris & Greg Talk	107
54.	Chris Quits	109
55.	Greg Quits	112
56.	Transparency	113
57.	Help	117
58.	Discovery Pays	118

59.	Finding Gold	119
60.	Quips	121
61.	Why Me?	122
62.	Where's the Beef?	124
63.	James Harness—In His Own Words	126
64.	Quartermaster General	129
65.	Top Ten List (of Risks)	131
66.	Commentary on the Top 10 List	132
67.	Life After	135
68.	Paranoia	138
69.	General Todd	139
70.	Metamorphosis	140
71.	Bad Taste In Their Mouth	141
72.	Hollywood	142
73.	Reality TV?	144
74.	Why Go With Gold Rush?	145
75.	Romney & Gold	146
76.	A Slip of A Lip	148
77.	Leaving Gold Rush	152
78.	Evictions	153
79.	After Gold Rush	154
80.	Mundane Living	156
81.	Idiosyncrasies	157
82.	James Disabled	169
83.	James Revisited	170
84.	Remembering	175
85.	How I Killed James	176
86.	Funeral Day	178
87.	Unfulfilled Plans	182
88.	Palm Springs	183
89.	Everybody Writes	185
90.	Lingering Issues	193
91.	Last Paragraph	193
92.	Swan Song	194
93.	Conclusion	195

94.	My 2 Cents	196
95.	2014 Christmas+1	197
96.	Epilogue	200
97.	Doubt Me? Author's Notes	201
98.	Glossary	204
99.	Photo Gallery	205

FOREWORD

Because of the untold incidents and events taking place in Oregon, Alaska and Canada, I decided to write this book chronologically. Good or bad, nothing will be held back. If Monday morning quarterbacking was allowed in the NFL, would I have undertaken this trip with a reality TV show and never "discover" what really went on? I'll let you be the judge. If opportunity knocked on your door, would you go? As for me, "Once a sucker, always a sucker."

DEDICATION

To Mom & Dad, the best parents anyone could ever have.
To James, for giving me the fortitude to write this book.

Thanks to GWAC for invaluable technical support.

INTRODUCTION

No duty or obligation precluded me in breaking my silence by writing this book. Because of an innocent, off the cuff remark about James Harness' character, I knew that it was time to set the record straight. I know James would have wanted me to write this book. And it was not for James' sake, but for his kids. Gold Rush was already behind him and he didn't care for it anymore; as he said, he had so much to live for the present.

Except to take occasional liberty to make a point, the following will be written pretty much in chronological (dis)order.

THESIS

Six unemployed men in the economically depressed Northwest are chasing the American Dream in a modern day gold rush in Alaska. With virtually no experience in mining, they sell whatever they have and go for broke. In the trek of their lives, will the six (seven) survive against the elements and themselves in their search for gold?

MY GOLD RUSH THESIS

This is no armchair general or Monday morning quarterback to expose the Gold Rush myth. I was there. Rode, ate, worked (a little) side by side with the cast members of the widely acclaimed and groundbreaking Discovery television reality show. A real gold strike for the Discovery Channel in its inaugural season, it was followed by more scintillating seasons which included new cast members working on different claims. I am restricting my discussions exclusively with those I associated with: Todd Hoffman's original group - Greg, James, Jim, Chris, Dave, Jack and Todd himself, of course. It is hoped that by sharing with you some of the most intimate and behind the scenes shots of what actually took place will reveal to you what reality is and is not. You be the judge.

Spinoffs from Todd's original Gold Rush show included Bering Sea Gold, Jungle Gold, Alaska(n) . . . you get the picture.

UNANSWERED QUESTIONS

Who has the gold?

Where did it go?

Why leave Alaska?

Are TV ratings more important than reality?

In the proverbial chicken or the egg coming first, is reality making the ratings or ratings making the reality?

Is it real or are they staging it to make it look real?

A kidnapping?

Going Hollywood?

Why are cast members revolting?

Investors, what investors?

Who financed a gold mining operation several thousands of miles away on a different continent?

Going to Africa, South America or nowhere?

How and why did Gold Rush's hero die?

Death of Gold Rush?

These are some of the questions and issues plaguing television's #1 hit Friday show for years and it finally gets answered here.

"A script, a director, actors…it's not the truth. It's one of the reasons today I laugh when I hear about reality television. Because the minute you put a camera in there, how real is it? It's totally faked from beginning to end."

> SIDNEY LUMET, award-winning film (and television) director of 12 ANGRY MEN, MURDER ON THE ORIENT EXPRESS, THE VERDICT, NETWORK, SERPICO, THE PAWNBROKER, and FAIL SAFE

"The thing we try to achieve was not to do a theatrical film, but a film about reality. This is the kind of reality that's important in motion pictures (television). If you try to act it, it doesn't quite come across as if you were really doing it."

> STEVE McQUEEN, one of the most popular actors ever

Under the guise of reality or more commonly called:
"THE TREASURE OF THE SIERRA MADRE"

The "Treasure of the Sierra Madre", the 1947 acclaimed movie and one of the most enduring masterworks produced (American Film Institute's American Movie Lists as the 30th greatest in 1998 and 67th most thrilling in 2001) is about two hard-luck drifters and a grizzled prospector seeking fortune and finding adventure, greed and paranoia. Each night, the experienced prospector weighed the gold mined that day and divided it up evenly between the three to keep. How's that for transparency? Why didn't any of Todd's group complain about this on or off camera? Can we draw similarities between reality and fiction? "You're all millionaires. All you have to do is to dig it up." The lure and the promise. Although this movie was not banned by Todd/RAW/Discovery from being shown to the cast members, it was frowned upon. Taken from the movie verbatim, can we see any parallels today? As the old prospector (Walter Huston) says:

"The question is, are you the right guy?
Real bonanzas are few and far between that take a lot of finding.
Why is gold worth so $20 an ounce?
A 1,000 men say go searching for gold. After 6 months one of them is lucky. One out of a thousand. His find represents not only his own labor but that of 999 others to boot. That's 6,000 months, 500 years scrambling over mountains going hungry and thirsty.
An ounce of gold is worth what it is because of the human labor that went into the finding and getting of it.
Gold is a devilish sort of thing anyway. You start out to tell yourself that you'll be satisfied with $25,000. So help me Lord. Cross my heart. Fine resolution. After months of sweating yourself dizzy and going short on provisions and finding nothing, you finally come down to 15,000, then 10,000. Finally, you say,
'Lord, let me find just $5,000 and I'll never ask for anything more for the rest of my life.'
To make a real strike you couldn't be dragged away. Not even the threat of miserable death to keep you from trying to add $10,000 more. 10,000 you get 25,000 and then 50,000, then 100,000. Like roulette, one more turn. You know, always one more. I know what gold does to men's soul.
Never knew a prospector who died rich. Make one fortune and blew it trying to make another."

BASICS

No machinery was needed save the simplest tools; no organization was required, beyond a willing partner; no capital, save muscle. - T.A. Rickard, 1909

Placer gold mining is the practice of separating heavily eroded gold from sand or gravel. The word placer is thought to have come from Catalan and Spanish, meaning a shoal or sand bar. The word entered the American vocabulary during the 1849 California Gold Rush, and when gold was discovered in Alaska and the Canadian Klondike in the Yukon in the 1890's, the gold-seekers brought with them various placer mining technologies. By far the simplest was the prospector's pan that worked by swirling a combination of water and gravel or sand and allowing the lighter, rocky material to spill out. Relying on the fact that gold is nineteen times heavier than water is the principle used in all placer mining operations.

The first challenge is to find a creek drainage that over the years carried gold dust, flakes and nuggets downward to be deposited in layers of creek sediments. To do this, prospectors used pans to test the surface gravels or dug straight down to a point just above bedrock where placer gold tends to collect. They then tunneled horizontally to follow the richest ground. This approach is called drift mining (the horizontal tunnel is the drift). These shafts and tunnels were typically dug in winter so that frozen ground would not melt and collapse on the miners. Even so, the practice was arduous and dangerous. In spring and summer, a defrosting pile of gold-rich gravel called pay dirt could be processed using the placer mining's best friend – water.

Utter contempt for the environment

      Miners can use a prospector's pan to collect their gold one pan at a time, but this is slow, backbreaking work. Every member of Todd's team, including yours truly, can testify how excruciating it can be. To speed up the process, they use the flow of water through wooden troughs called sluice boxes. In the bottom of the box a series of riffles, like shallow fences, agitate the slurry of water and gravel, encouraging small particles of gold to fall out of the solution (again, because they are heavier than sand and rock). In this way, gold can be captured while the waste material spills out of the end of the box. As an alternative to building lengthy sluice boxes on site, some early placer miners carried with them mobile sluicing units called rockers (compact, boxy sluices operated by rocking the unit side to side) and long-toms (a portable sluice box that did not need to be built on site).

One - man operation

Sluicing

GOLD PRICE

When the worldwide appetite of gold made it hit around $1,700 an ounce in 2011, I reminded Todd the market collapsed when the prices of gold and oil surged on strong emerging market demand and supply issues in the 1990's. He believes inflation and the uncertainty of the economy for the continued rise. By citing Goldman Sachs' 2011 technical report of gold retreating back to the high $1,000's and the low $1,100's (prevailing price to mine an ounce of gold) [which was not well taken by Todd], it cited the long-term price of gold should remain steady in a trading channel of $1,000 - 1,300, pending unforeseen political and/or economic calamity. I again reminded Todd of the historical consumption of gold, which goes in fundamental cycles. For example, China and India, two of the world's biggest gold buyers, will have reduced purchases from 350 tons in 2005 to 150 tons currently, a 60% drop. Because of the end of the super cycle for commodities since 2011, the long-term trend remains decidedly against gold. With the U.S. dollar remaining strong versus the yen, euro and other currencies and with the Federal Reserve talking about raising rates again (possibly twice more in 2018), that trend is assuredly going to continue. At the same time, emerging-market demand has been soft. Lastly, it cites the steady erosion of gold being used as a storehouse of wealth in lieu of higher interest-bearing instruments and other financial equities over the next five years (2016 Presidential election). Dow Jones has surged beyond the 26,000 stratosphere.

The all too important 18-49 sophisticated age group are changing their spending and consuming habits. The millennial generation is changing its fashion tastes from gold to white metals such as platinum and palladium. Jewelry demand remains weak worldwide. As a result, don't commit yourself long-term because the glitter of gold may soon fade along with the need for gold as a storehouse for wealth and currency devaluation.

However, argument can be made for the demand for gold when this or any other commodity can be propped up by falling prices. Many central banks remain buyers of gold. Countries like Russia look to gold in propping up its currency. Because gold has been beaten down too far, buyers may be able to swoop in large part because of how cheap the precious metal had become in the eyes of buyers. All this may add up to short-term potential for gold, even if long-term price targets don't hold a lot of upside. Quantitative easing in Japan favors the U.S. dollar, and a stronger dollar means weaker prices for commodities such as gold that are pegged in and to U.S. dollars. Rekindling interest in gold as an investment alternative may become more difficult as geopolitics have moved to the back burner leading investors to lose interest in troubles abroad. A lot of commodity experts believe a direct investment in gold bullion will not give you reliable returns over the next few years.

With the broader pressure against gold to continue, the long-term view for gold remains weak. Altogether, the lower demand for gold may dampen audience appeal in watching a gold themed show.

GOT MONEY?

In the first season's last episode, Todd makes a plea for help of an investor. Not knowing the full ramifications or implications of this solicitation, I decided to call Monday, reaching the Sandy Airport and leaving a message for Jack or Todd Hoffman. This call was returned shortly thereafter. After exchanging some pleasantries with Jack, an appointment was made for me to come up to meet with them. Realizing this mining operation didn't appear to be that profitable on the bottom line, I did not expect some sort of significant return on the investment, just something reasonable like a simple percentage with return on principal. Whenever I represent myself or a group of investors, reputation generally precedes me, i.e., my door opener. In this case, I've never undertaken an endeavor like this before. Due diligence is generally made on the borrower or investee on a case by case basis followed by interviews and final screening. My legal department secures mutual agreement by parole evidence before proper and prompt funds disbursement.

My door opener in this situation was an antique walking stick with a gold handle and inscriptions from the San Francisco 1849 California Gold Rush era for Jack (he reminded me of being dapper like Fred Astaire), a couple of cases of Ghirardelli chocolate for members of the show/team, and a case of plush Beanie Babies animal toys for Todd's daughter.

Looking back at the very beginning, I had difficulty in getting to downtown the hotel to meet with Todd the next morning, so I called him for directions. What I got was a ridiculous set of directions taking me all over the map of northern Oregon; it took me on side roads and appeared to be a maze. Finally, I flagged down a state trooper and got: 5-205-84 and the main street in rather quick order.

Eight hours later, a phone call from Todd brought me out of the hotel with him awaiting inside his big F350 pickup. I took the gifts out of my car's trunk and loaded them behind me in his truck's rear seat. Not knowing what to expect, Todd and I exchanged pleasantries while we meandered down a narrow canyon road to the valley floor. Upon arrival at the lodge (large auditorium with sporting, hunting and fishing trophies), I was greeted by Jack and the very first words out of his mouth were:

"Gold Rush is being made for the purpose of reaching the lost for Christ."

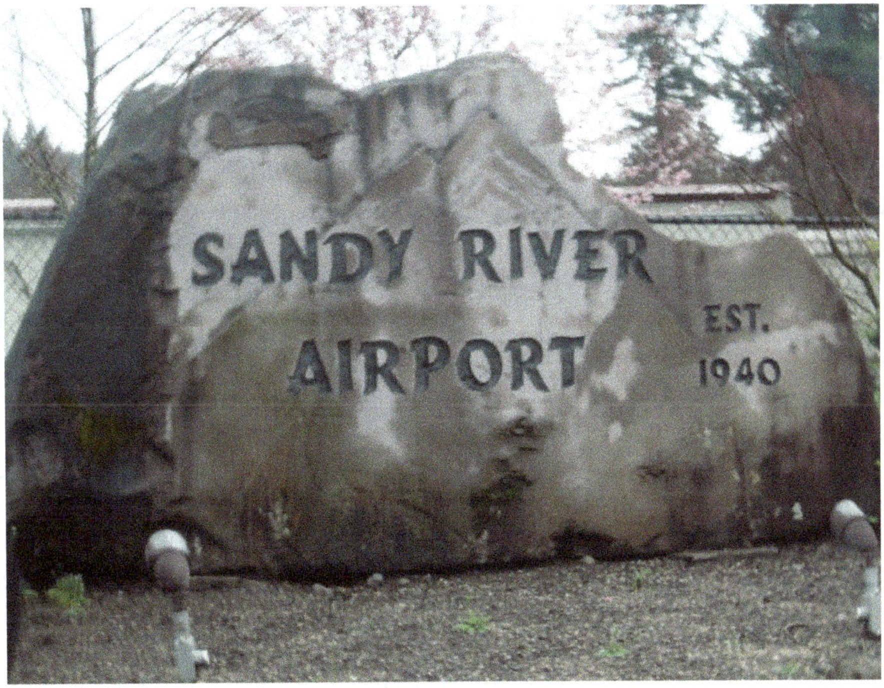
SANDY RIVER
AIRPORT
EST.
1940

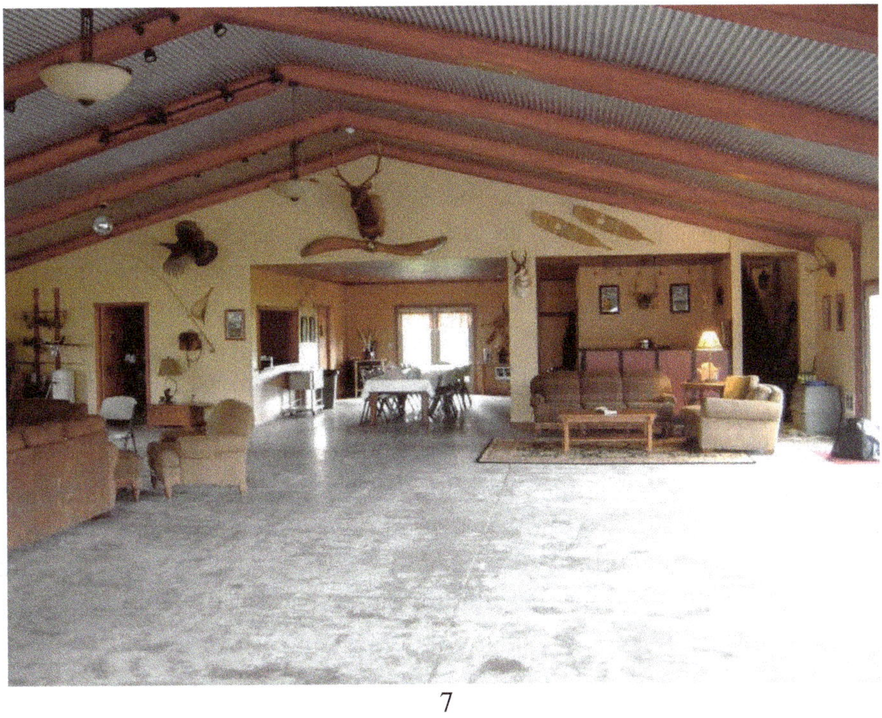

They each professed their faith to carry out the Bible's Great Commission. I had more than an inclination that this (business/proposal) meeting was going to lead up to this area of discussion since viewing an episode of men praying together. Realizing that we share similar beliefs, they explained that they wanted to use this show as a ministry to reach people for Christ and also to "infiltrate" Hollywood with God's message. I was taken back with the use of the word "infiltrate" since it has a negative connotation when used in the military sense.

Minutes later, Greg Remsburg enters the lodge and he also gives a hearty handshake.

We all immediately found common ground in faith. Normally, any businessman's jaw would just drop to the floor. I could tell from a business standpoint that the Hoffmans have received more than a few rejections from other prospective investors. When watching episodes of Gold Rush in its maiden season, I saw examples of prayer and similar rhetoric being made, despite select editing by RAW and/or Discovery. It wasn't the adventure of an Alaskan landscape nor the "real life" drama of men struggling to put food on their family's table but the sincerity of each individual not being ashamed of who they are and what they stood for. I've seen this played out in the lives of our military here and abroad and with homeless veterans in many communities across our nation. Recognizing this as our common roots, I empathized with Todd and Jack's need to fulfill their mission. Further enthusiasm on both sides of the aisle prompted me to return to the discussion table at a later date. I left Oregon and proceeded to drive home when I received a call to return.

Back at the Sandy Airport, Mike Fox, their business associate, joined us to discuss their investment need of another project called BATTLEGROUND. Instead of providing a business plan or a written proposal, a white chalk board hastily written with a marker pen showed funding needs for filming a pilot on mixed martial arts overseas (Europe). Again, a passionate plea is being made to use this show to fulfill the Great Commission. Moreover, Todd especially wanted to also use this show as a platform to "infiltrate" Hollywood. According to Merriam Webster, the definition of infiltrate is "a method of attack in which small groups of soldiers . . . penetrate into the enemy's line in order to assemble behind the enemy's position", aka Germans at the Battle of the Bulge, Communist Chinese at the 35th Parallel, and the North Vietnamese at the Tet Offensive. Despite a lot of arm twisting, I took this latest suggestion under advisement. Even though the dollar figures were relatively modest when compared with today's major television budgets, it was an area that these men had relatively no experience nor were they risking any financial interests themselves. In other words, it was just a concept. Notwithstanding any financial investment on Gold Rush as discussed earlier, the table was now turned towards an ancillary television concept with no track record of itself nor anybody save for Todd's. He held a significant percentage of what was called the Bonhoeffer Boys Limited

Liability Partnership.

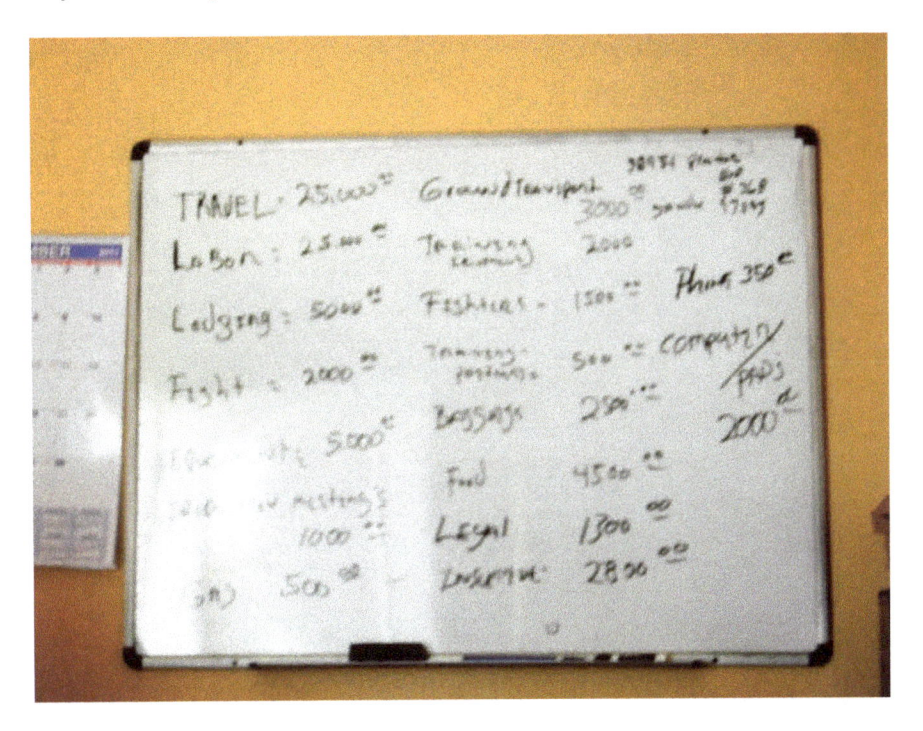

Bonhoeffer Boys LLC's namesake came from Dietrich Bonhoeffer, a German Lutheran pastor, theologian and anti-Nazi dissident who vocally opposed Hitler's euthanasia program and genocidal persecution of the Jews. Bonhoeffer was arrested in April 1943 by the Gestapo and imprisoned at Tegal Prison for one and a half years before being transferred to a Nazi concentration camp. After being allegedly associated with the plot to assassinate Adolph Hitler, he was briefly tried along with other accused plotters, and then executed by hanging on April 9, 1945 as the Nazi regime collapsed, just three weeks before Hitler's suicide.

Riding on the back of Todd's success with Gold Rush, the other partners included Mike Fox and U.S. Olympian gold medal-destined wrestler Dan Russell, the featured star of the show.

BATTLEGROUND's premise is a modern day version of the student-teacher relationship as portrayed by the 1970's "KUNG FU" show conceived by Bruce Lee but starred David Carradine (no offense taken, Academy Award winner Keith).

BONHOEFFER BOYS LLC
P.O. Box 1016 Sandy, Oregon 97055

Name:
Address:
Date:

Dear Name:

Battleground ("the Production")

This letter is to confirm the terms on which we are prepared to disclose/discuss the details of the Production to/with you.

For the purposes of this letter 'Confidential Information' means all information of whatever nature in whatever form relating to the Production obtained from any source including without limitation information received from Bonhoeffer Boys LLC (the Company) and information obtained as a result of being allowed access to any premises where the Company may carry on business but does not extend to information obtained in the public domain.

You agree as follows:

You shall treat all Confidential Information as being strictly private and confidential and shall take all steps necessary to prevent it from being disclosed or made public to any third party or coming by any means into the possession of any third party.

You shall use the Confidential Information solely for the purpose of evaluating whether or not to enter into an agreement with the Company relating to the Production or to perform any obligations which you may undertake or have undertaken with the Company relating to the Production and you shall not use any part of the Confidential Information for any other purpose whatsoever.

You shall not use or disclose or permit the disclosure by any person of the Confidential Information for the benefit of any third party or in such a way as to procure a commercial advantage over the Company.

The Confidential Information and its circulation shall be restricted to circulation and disclosure to individuals whose identity shall have been approved by the Company prior to disclosure in writing.

You shall keep all materials containing Confidential Information in a safe and secure place and return them to the Company immediately on determination of our discussions in relation to the Production or on the Company's request.

You undertake to indemnify and keep the Company at all times fully indemnified from and against any loss or disclosure of Confidential Information and from all actions proceedings claims demands costs awards and damages however arising as a result of any breach or non-performance of any of the warranties undertakings or obligations under this agreement.

Sincerely,

(signature on behalf of Company)

(signature of owner)
I agree and confirm the above and to be bound by it.

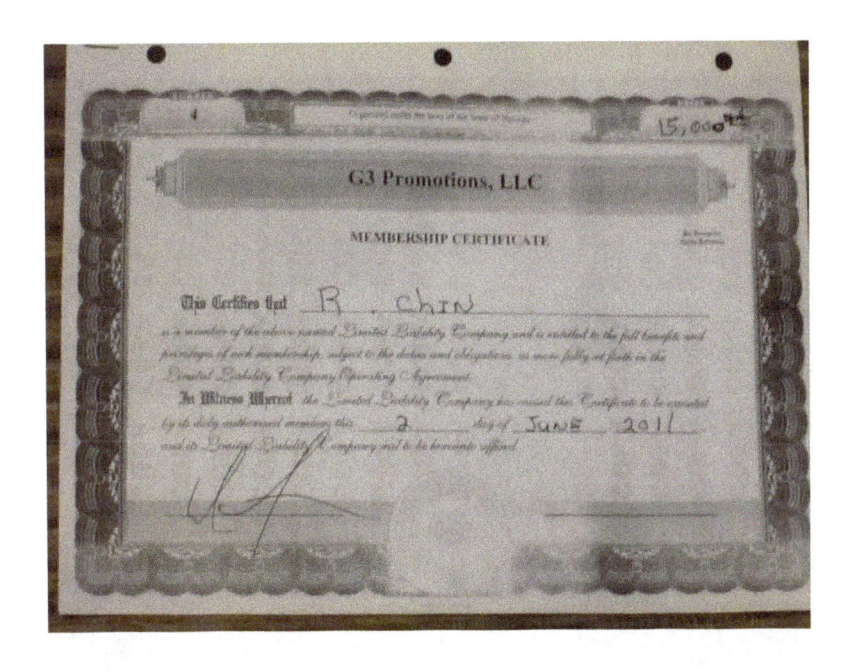

Keith Carradine

It was well known that ABC Television took KUNG FU away from Bruce Lee and handed the torch to David Carradine. Dan Russell was intended to guide the Mixed Martial Arts (MMA) student in his quest to become a champion.

Because of its namesake in Washington state, the town of Battle Ground has been the "breeding" and training ground of some of the greatest wrestlers and fighters in the world.

12

This triune partnership of Bonhoeffer Boys LLC eventually quartered equally when Todd convinced me to fund it. In essence, when Todd deemed to have sufficient investment capital at the end of season one for a second mining season, whether factual or fictitious, Todd turned to apply these additional, newly acquired funds to a shell with no financial or real assets. With the capital infusion I provided, it eventually became a four-way, coequal partnership. Monies were used to finance filming overseas and post production as well. Because of Todd's success through Gold Rush, it was believed that Todd would garner enough influence to have a leg up in promoting and exploiting BATTLEGROUND.

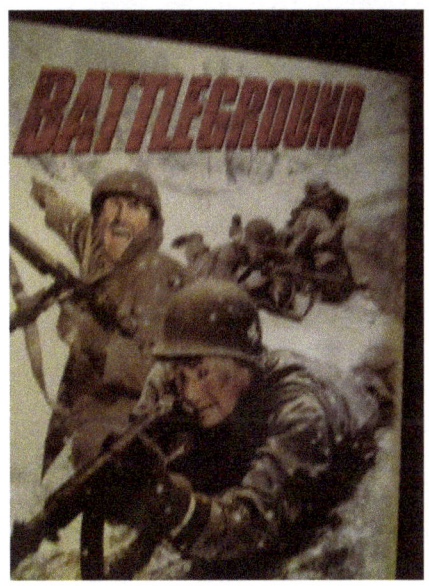

Opportunity was offered for me to accompany them (and appear) in filming the fight sequences overseas. Since it required me to pay my own expenses, I politely turned down the offer and later chose to accept the Hoffman's invitation to accompany the cast of Gold Rush to Alaska, the last state I have yet to visit in the Union.

GIVING GOOD GIFTS

Giving gifts has many motives. It can open doors or it can be a way of showing gratitude. To say nothing in the least, it can be a way of showing who the giver is. And, giving a gift should have no strings attached whatsoever. What gift can one give to someone who appears to have everything? This dilemma usually shows up annually on someone's birthday, anniversary or Christmas.

In the early morning of the first week of June 1974, I was readying for breakfast in Solvang, California (Danish capital of America). I looked outside my hotel room and saw a caravan of black GMC SUVs in the midst of parking a block away. A moment later, a CHP (California Highway Patrol) motorcade followed. With my eyes wide open, I saw one of my favorite movie stars come out of a limo. Gen. Jimmy Stewart was awaiting for the next limo to drop off the next luminary. With his right hand extended, another distinguished gentleman came out of his limo and took Stewart's hand - Gov. Ronald Reagan. Needless to say, this is one encounter I will never forget and it would certainly not to be the last.

To show my appreciation for the leadership he gave to this country, and for the opportunities of exchanging more than a few platitudes with me, I had the opportunity of giving a gold placard in Chinese characters to the Reagans.

For the President and First Lady

In a small reception for ABC News anchor Diane Sawyer at the Reagan Library, private residential quarters, in Simi Valley, California, I saw that gold placard given to the Reagans earlier, placed along with other gifts from friends and dignitaries around the world.

Congressman Dana Rohrabacher invited me to a luncheon with about 20 guests for Arnold Schwarzenegger. Again, the indelible question of what to give to someone who has everything —a beautiful family, an Ohio shopping center, $800 million and an occasional acting job (before T-3). After giving a 30+ minute impromptu talk followed by a Q & A session (all without a teleprompter), I gave him a glass box encasing a gold placard in Chinese characters with some personal remarks thanking him for supporting our military, a couple of Navy SEAL tee-shirts (way too small for him but it was the biggest size I could get at the Coronado PX) and a book personally inscribed to Arnold from former White House Deputy Chief of Staff, Michael Deaver, *A Different Drummer: My Thirty Years with Ronald Reagan*. Deaver writes about Reagan's battle with Alzheimer's and says it's Nancy Reagan's "finest hour", a validation of the greatest love story he has ever known. Mr. Deaver was kind enough to send that to me on very short notice. Very shortly thereafter (days later), private-citizen Arnold appeared on Jay Leno's Tonight Show making the announcement to run for governor. It was not long thereafter (3/20/02) that Arnold gave a beautiful gold sculpture bust of the 40th President by the late sculptor Robert Berks; it now sits on the second floor in the private living quarters of the Reagan Library Museum.

Arnold Schwarzenegger's gift to the Reagans

In addition to using Reaganism throughout his candidacy and office as Governor(nator), I like to believe that my recent gifts to Arnold inspired him to give that sculpture - but you'll have to ask him.

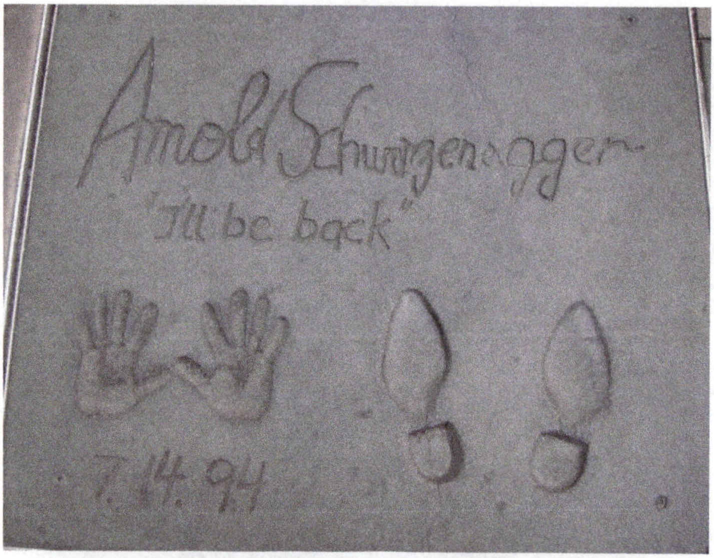
Arnold Schwarzenegger
"I'll be back"
7. 14. 94

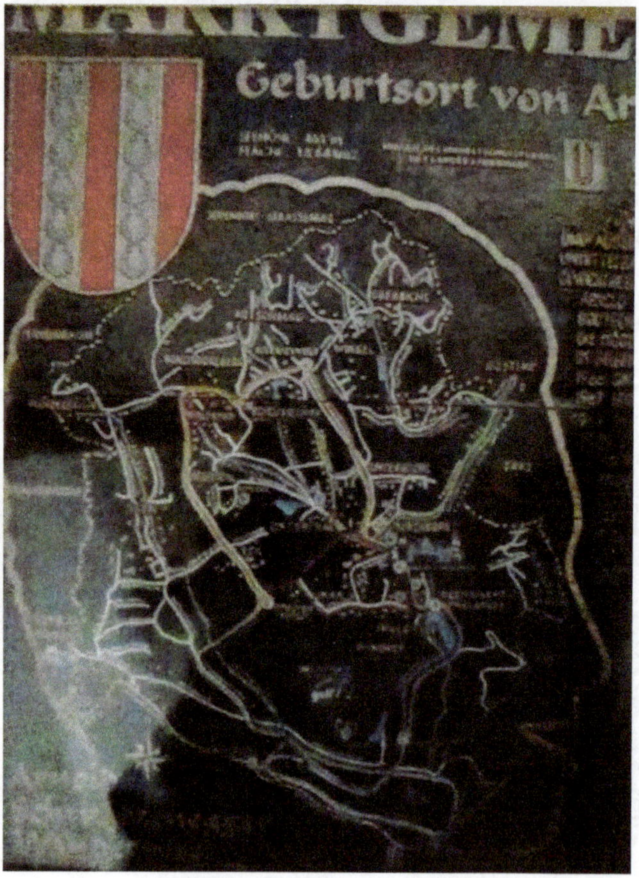
Geburtsort von Ar

For the soon to be Governator

In my continuing desire to give good gifts to someone who has everything (Jack Hoffman who has a great family, an airport and a dog named Blue), I turned to Deric Torres of Clars Auction Gallery. Without hesitation, he told me to give Jack a real artifact from the 1849 California Gold Rush. It was a historic gold cane, most befitting a debonair man who walks the Barbary Coast with a certain air of distinction.

In reality, I was a fan of Teddy Roosevelt's "Talk soft but carry a big 'stick'" diplomacy.

Big Stick Diplomacy

I don't have to tell you the reaction I got from giving that gift.

TV STRATEGY

    Todd admitted to me that he doesn't know a lot about many things. But Todd declared that he does know television, at least from the standpoint of keeping audiences suspended week to week as in serials of past generations ("Flash Gordon" - movies, "24" - TV). To structure his Gold Rush show into a serial, Todd offered little gold production success in its inaugural season, better gold production in the second season, a climatic, great third season, only to be followed with a new cycle preceding a throwaway fourth season. Here is a simplistic illustration:

ratings based on gold yields

```
            2010   2011   2012   2013   2014   2015   2016
ratings _____
        _____
        _____X_____
        _____X_____
        _____X_____X_____
        _____X_____
        _____X_____
season    1      2      3      4      5      6      7
         Alaska Alaska Yukon South  Yukon  Yukon  Oregon
               +Yukon       America
```

gold mined in oz. (est.)

Todd	9	96	840	0	1,300	3,000
Fred		80	160	300	–	–
Parker		50	200	1,000	2,500	3,400

23

GRAPHIC SUCCESS

This is how Todd plans for the success of Gold Rush on TV, as he told me.

```
Au _____
                                                    ?
 s _____X_____
 u _____X_____
 c _____
 c _____X_____
 e _____X_____
 s ___X_____
 s _____X_____

   Season   1       2       3       4       5       6       7
          Alaska  Alaska/ Yukon  Guyana  Yukon   Yukon   Oregon
                  Yukon
```

    To reiterate Todd's TV strategy as he relayed it to me: Little success in the first season as they struggle, some success in the second season, and great success in the third season - then repeat this strategy over a cycle of three more seasons after a throwaway season (South America). This is his formula for achieving TV success.

    Todd says he knows TV. To seize, captivate, and hold the audience is like fishing for shark. You lure the shark with bait, first with a little and then more as the blood scent becomes more intensified. In the first season, Todd had to create something that most people could relate to. For example, in about 99.44% of local, state and national elections, you need to inject the notion of "the economy" to get voters stirred up. To win the election, remind everyone: "It's the economy, stupid." People's lives are centered around their jobs so that they can support themselves and their families. We all have to eat and we all have to have jobs. This responsibility is foremost in everyone's mind. You don't have to look far if not under your own roof - just pull your kitchen window curtains back and see your next door neighbor in this predicament. It has been said (by Reagan) that it's a recession when your neighbor is out of a job. It's a depression when you're out of a job. A lot of people from 2009 were out of jobs or (still) underemployed and (still) under paid. The country has suffered significant unemployment and many pockets of the country, like Oregon and rural America, are still reeling and have yet to recover.

    Todd's idea of making and shopping around a short video "pilot" he shot was nothing less than a real amateur job, according to some Gold Rush cast members. Never knowing the number of rejections, RAW eventually picked it up and as they usually say, "the rest is history."

Finding six men and families in rural Sandy, Oregon wasn't hard to fit the bill. The assembling of the trek, the course of the trek and eventually arriving at the end of the rainbow in Alaska made for good drama.

All Todd wanted for the first season, at least in front of the camera, a little success in getting gold so that the audience wants to come back for more, something liken in the old days, a serial. Ask the older generation when they paid a nickel at their local bijou week after week to see how the plot thickens as the hero survives a cliffhanger fall. Continuing the melodramatic adventure into the second season was to pursue and get better mining success. The third season was to be the coup de grace, the big kill to end the three year pursuit. Mission accomplished. A stupid old movie line/statement like "Hi o silver" from "The Lone Ranger" (Clayton Moore) or "holy moly" from Batman's Robin (Burt Ward). Todd needs seven years for syndication of the Gold Rush show. Why not "Ghana, Africa" as Chris repeated it back to Todd - "no, Guyana, South America." The stage was set, or was it? Jim Thurber corroborates it to be a one shot season down there and unsustainable for any longer length than that (to be discussed later in the book). Well, after season seven, the ball keeps rolling and the cycle repeats. The audience's short attention span has already kicked in, as evidenced in the ratings. Discovery re-signs Chris again and hopes another Lazarus would be raised. "The only thing man learns from history is that man does not learn from history", attributable to historian Arnold Toynbee.

AUCTION

When Todd needed to purchase a dozer for the show, he and everyone else went to the Ritchie Brothers Auction in nearby Troutdale, Oregon.

When I arrived with intentions to assist, Greg welcomed me but asked for my purpose of attending. I previewed the heavy equipment the day before and registered for the auction bidding placard the following day. When I bumped into Mike Fox, he accompanied me to sit under the make-shift tent in front of the auctioneer and waited for select dozers to come up for bidding. With RAW filming the auction proceedings, Todd bid early and low to no avail. I left the tent to get a better view of the heavy equipment rolling in. After the good dozers were taken by higher bidders, leaving nothing for him, I saw Todd leaving the tent. Not realizing what he was doing, I saw him in the reflection of

the plastic tent window sneaking up behind me. Todd grabbed me in a bear hug. At first I held back in executing my instincts, namely to stomp his foot, break the hold and throw him over my shoulder. I knew the ground was hard and both the crowd and RAW were present. So rather than have Todd land on his head and back and possibly get scraped or injured, and therefore have my invitation to Alaska rescinded, I let him have his moment of glory and played along.

INVITING KATO

What really prompted Todd to invite Kato on this trip? Well, I was supposed to be an investor of the show - Todd made a sweeping solicitation for help on the first season's last episode. No one made any mention of me being on the show. During discussions, the investee (Todd) was doing due diligence on the investor (Kato). I said, "Shouldn't it be the other way around?" The bank interviews the borrower, not the borrower who interviews the bank.

After further discussions and verbal agreements were concluded, we began to relax and went clockwise around the table sharing some recent experiences that might be interesting. When my turn came up, I mentioned that I'd been to forty countries, including a recently concluded journey of visiting 6 continents in 6 months. I told them that I was actually going to make it 7 continents in 7 months but a major earthquake on a tip of South America precluded me (and most travelers) from visiting Antarctica at that time. Besides, I said, "There will be the next time." In the same breath, I told Todd and Jack that I frequently visit every state in the Union, except for one. Of course, they didn't have to ask me which state. By my own choosing, I told them that I had never used a tour guide on any of my overseas trips - it was the adventurous side of me. It was not too long thereafter that they invited me to accompany me on the Gold Rush trek to Alaska. I didn't have to think a nanosecond about accepting.

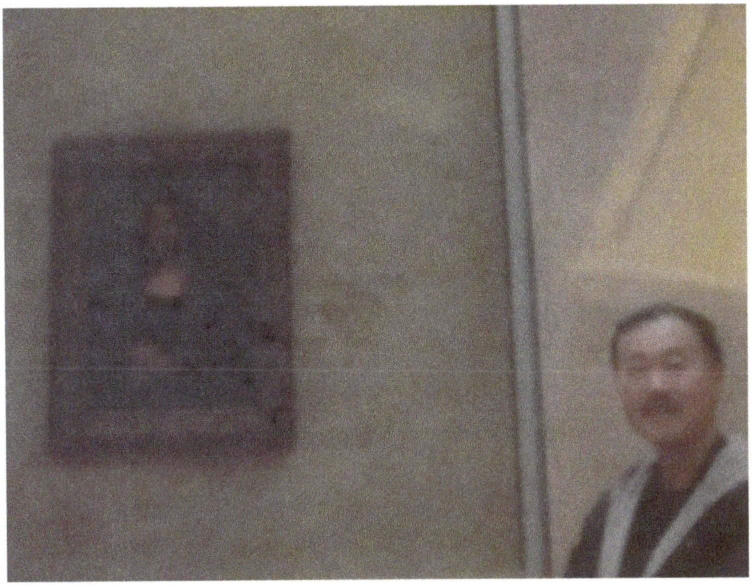

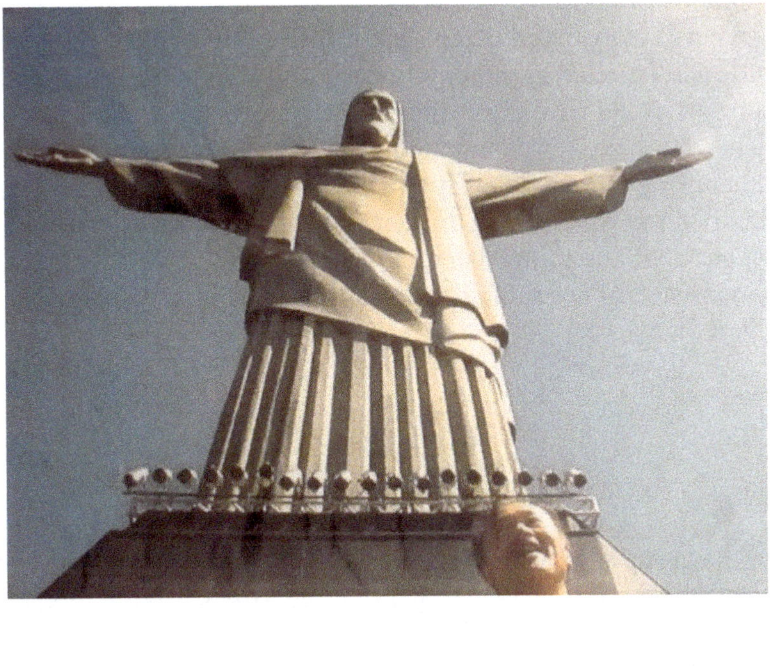

SUCKERED

During season one, claims on television were continuously made that Jim Thurber's home mortgage delinquency was about to go into effect. It never went into default. When I fell for this claim of Jim failing to bring his mortgage current, I asked James Harness to help find a suitable truck for Jim. James screened and found several candidates, negotiated the best price, purchased it and performed a top to bottom preventive maintenance and overhaul before relinquishing it to me to give to Jim. I suggested and James acquiesced to perform preventive maintenance on everyone's truck before leaving on this trek. Unlike the first season, we didn't want to spend an entire episode focused on a dead battery or a flat tire again. Under the circumstances, James burned the midnight candle in finishing this task.

Greg later asked me for a couple of thousand dollars for new tires for his truck. I guess he thought I was a walking ATM.

MIDNIGHT WALKER

On the night before leaving the Sandy Airport for Alaska, I was "sleeping" in the auditorium/lodge but in actuality was standing guard. A few minutes past midnight, I saw movement outside and I circled around in the dark and behind the "intruder." With a Mag-Lite, I lit up Mrs. Todd Hoffman who was carrying boxes to Todd's RV. As she entered, she stashed her boxes of dehydrated health foods in one of the RV compartments. I helped her bring more inside. By this action, plans have already been made for her to visit Todd up in the gold mining district.

Sidebar note. I vividly remembered a lunch that she made subsequently at their airport home. It consisted of a scrumptious salad followed by a delicious pasta - a lot of TLC went into it.

LEAVING SANDY AIRPORT

To avoid the group shot being filmed by RAW, I stood behind the cameramen before Todd gave the order for his men to get into their trucks. With Todd taking point and James positioned to pick up stragglers, Todd gave the signal and then I climbed into James' truck. The caravan circled around the airport grounds twice (didn't get the first shot right?). It was like a wagon train circling for an Indian attack that headed out before leaving loved ones in Sandy behind. With adrenaline high, enthusiastic chatter between everyone's walkie-talkies (furnished, and monitored by RAW?) weren't tempered until we reached the Washington state line. I wished everyone could have seen James whooping it up in his cab.

You know, it's rare to find a man who likes talking to a man who likes to talk. James fit that bill and I hope that the feeling was mutual.

With hundreds of miles of monotonous driving behind us, Todd interjects his walkie-talkie with quips and jokes at everything and everyone. When the subject matter became less clever, Todd turned to picking names or handles to call each other – nothing derogatory or disparaging, but just for fun. I'm sure it was also meant to keep everyone on their toes. There's no room for miscues in pulling heavily laden RVs with RAW watching and filming. When my turn came up, I said that you can call me by my first name ___. At that time (I guess all the time) they thought that I was a straight shooter lacking any sense of humor. Already acquainted with Todd, Jack, James, and Jim somewhat, Todd wanted to break the ice with some of the other team members and RAW to explain why this Asian guy was accompanying them. It's not hard in second guessing what they were probably thinking:

"Who is this guy, what does he want, and why is he here? What's he bringing to the table?" (besides cookies & confections).

At the airport, Discovery demanded signed waivers and confidentiality agreements from me numerous times. Despite complying with their requests, they kept after me for more. Finally, I said, "I am here at the invitation of Todd and Jack and I serve at their pleasure." Most, if not all the guys, stood behind me despite Discovery's insistence.

Some of the guys who saw the equipment, tools, food supplies, hygiene and medical items that I brought (which were all necessary for the maintenance and operation of a military command - logistics) didn't quite understand my motive. Maybe they thought I overstepped my boundary when I provided each member of the team a confidential "check list" sheet to be completed in case of medical emergencies. I later learned while up at the Yukon that Dave's wife is a RN. We recalled the emergency medical protocol was woefully lacking during the first season; for example, Todd's daughter in a respiratory seizure and James and others with bruises and contusions. If I had anything to say about anything as important as the welfare of the men, I knew that repetition of the mistakes made in the first season weren't going to happen under my watch. Emergency solar lighting, solar-heated showers and water purification systems were also brought by me to address those problems that occurred.

James did succeed in making me crack a smile when a joke was blurted out that made sense to me. Todd thought of _____ as my handle or nickname. I said in my mind, "Is he a racist?" Jim suggested _____. Jack's was more practical with _____. I said why not. With Jack's military background, I thought it was rather clever and well-suited. After a long pause James, squeezed his walkie-talkie and announced to everyone "K-A-T-O." I don't remember whether it was Todd or Chris who joked at that name since the Pink Panther's Burt Kwock character was portrayed as the butt of jokes and slander by Peter Seller's Inspector Clouseau. That movie series shamefully painted the name of Kato. I grabbed James' walkie-talkie and explained to everyone that the late, great Bruce Lee proudly wore the mantle of Kato. I also reminded everyone that people who watched the "Green Hornet" television show in Hong Kong, Bruce Lee's second home (his birthplace was San Francisco), called it the "Kato Show." James shook my hand (actually I grabbed his) and agreed with appropriateness that it was a proud name to strive for.

Whenever we stopped to refuel the guys and trucks, fans flocked to the cast members for photos and autographs. Everyone's ample supply of group photos was quickly depleted and RAW had Discovery make more, usually in different editions and reprints.

With Todd giving out Gold Rush photos to fans wherever we went, I suggested that in addition to signing his name that he write a short anecdote like his father's "NO GUTS, NO GLORY." I recommended John 3:16. As they say, the rest is history. On some occasions, Todd asked me to sign my name as well. I respectfully declined. With a little bit more arm twisting, I signed it only twice - one signed "KATO" and the other time with my name in Chinese characters. Whomever has them in Alaska or British Columbia, I make herein a standing offer to buy those two back for a "slight premium" and then I'll sequester them for posterity reasons (deep six).

As we were trucking along, I could tell when James was thinking to himself. He asked me if the Bible as we have it today is considered reliable. Translation-wise, I cited the oldest manuscripts that we have today, including the recent 1948 discovery of the Dead Sea scrolls, were almost verbatim (except for only a handful of different punctuation) to what we have today. Those Jewish scribes were so exacting in painstakingly transcribing one page, the whole sheet would be discarded and started over again if they made the slightest error. There were thousands of copies made as compared to the barely few of the Odyssey and the Iliad (in fragmentary form). This was just one example we discussed freely and intellectually.

Nearing the Canadian border, James politely asked if I minded listening to tape music he brought. I welcomed it. "What kind do you like", he asked. I said almost anything. He then played some of his own compositions that he recorded in cassette form. I sincerely said outstanding. I told him that I don't possess any musical talent after taking lessons for piano and guitar back in the dark ages. That led to his suggestion of forming another band of his own; he asked whether I have an interest. I said parole evidence it in the form of a business plan, which he did a year and a half later. Ultimately, James wanted to compose, assemble and tour with his own band. - We need more spirited individuals like him today.

JAMES' GHOST

I don't believe that my presence at Gold Rush was for filming purposes. In fact, I shunned all camera recordings of myself whenever they were shooting in the area. When the incident of Dave Turin flaring up was about to ignite, RAW followed and filmed me as I was doing a little work in connection with Wayne's wash plant. Whenever I saw them pointing the camera at me, I in turn pointed my rear posterior in that direction.

A group shoot that included everyone was taking place that morning as we departed the Sandy Airport. Everybody and anybody got in for the shot except myself, who shied away and retired behind the cameramen. Then the moment of departure arrived; the caravan formed. Todd said for everyone to jump into their trucks and follow him. I climbed into James' dually (3500 GMC with four rear wheels), the last vehicle in the wagon train - James' idea of being the rescue-emergency truck. We followed Todd as he circled twice (staging a second shot for RAW in case they missed the first take?). After the season premiered, we all saw that Kato was "blanked out" or removed from the departure scene with James - as if he was riding alone in his vehicle. However, RAW or Discovery didn't do a really good job of showing that scene since the outline of a person remained. Many people saw that outline next to James and thought it was a "ghost."

KATO REINCARNATED

KATO - how did we come up with this name? As mentioned, I decided to ride up with James, although Jack invited me to accompany him. I worked with Jack a little here and a little there before the trip, so we're amicable. Therefore, to share our faith with James, it was a good reason to accompany him. Riding in the high country, the guys conversed over the mikes provided by RAW. I'm sure everything was overheard. Todd wanted me to have a nickname like everyone else. Everyone put in their 2 cents worth. Without success from the other guys, James suggested Kato. They all laughed. I reminded them that it was Bruce Lee who played in the 1966/7 Green Hornet television show, the trusted sidekick/houseboy/protector/protege of Britt Reid (Van Williams).

So it was agreed to use Kato as my call-name, handle or nickname. Unbeknownst to the guys was the fact that there were many similarities drawn from Bruce Lee: born in San Francisco, resided in the Bay Area, was friends with Greglon Lee (Greglon's father, James, taught Bruce Wing Chun and Bruce taught JKD - Jeet Kune Do - to James and

Greglon), trained with JKD students, met Linda (Lee), Bruce Cadwell and Shannon Lee in Los Angeles, and friends trained directly under Bruce.

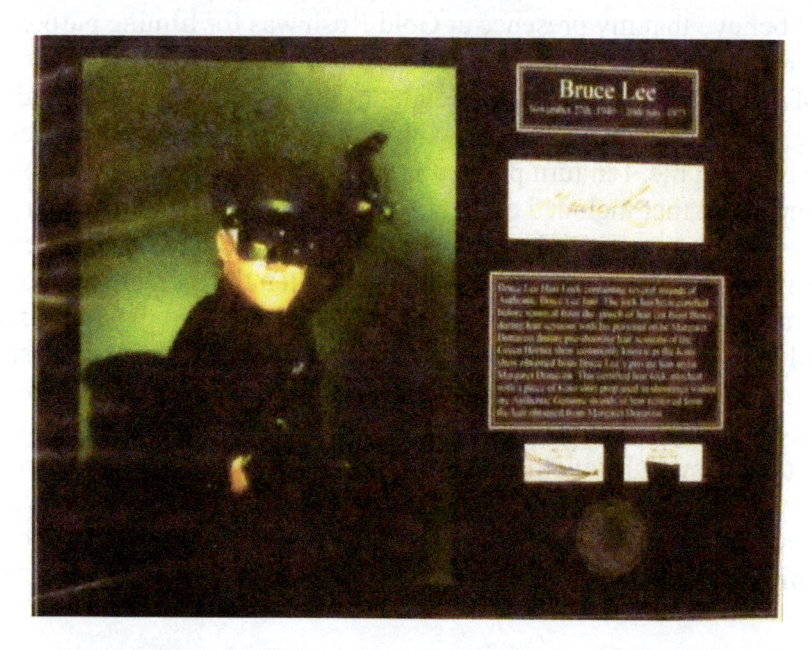

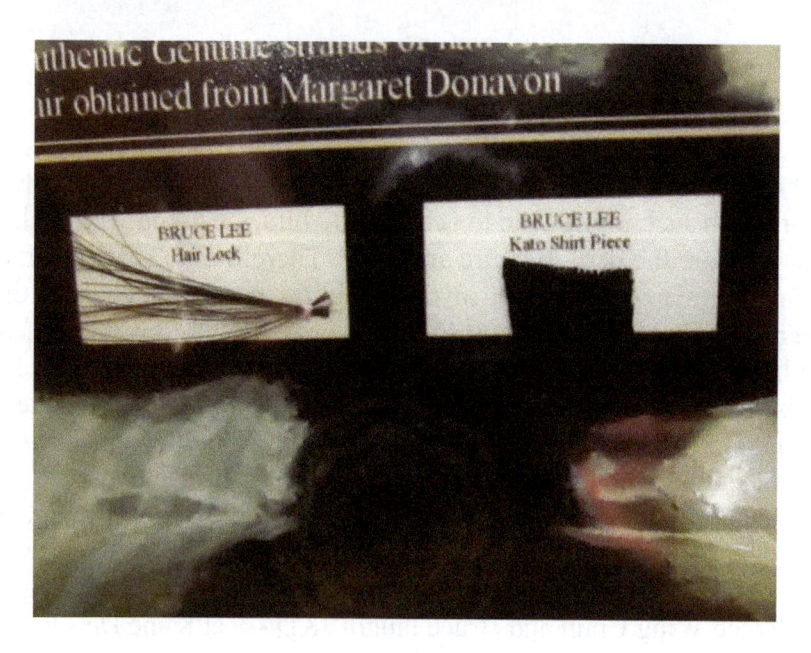

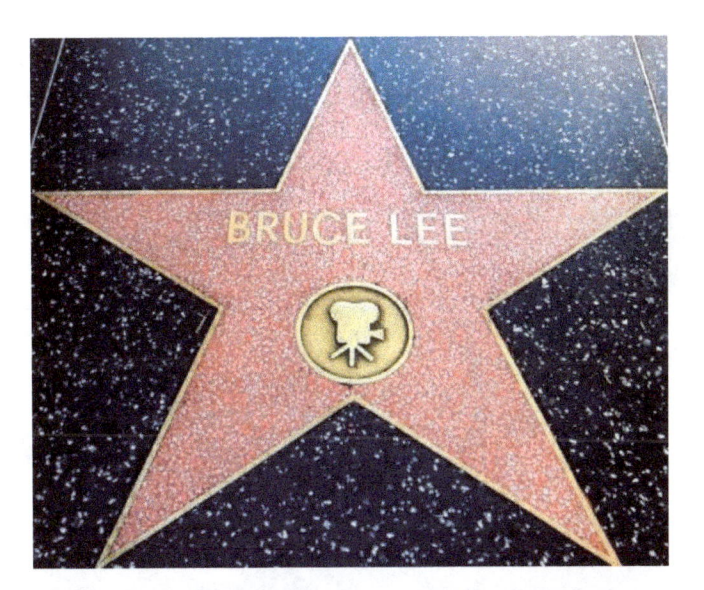

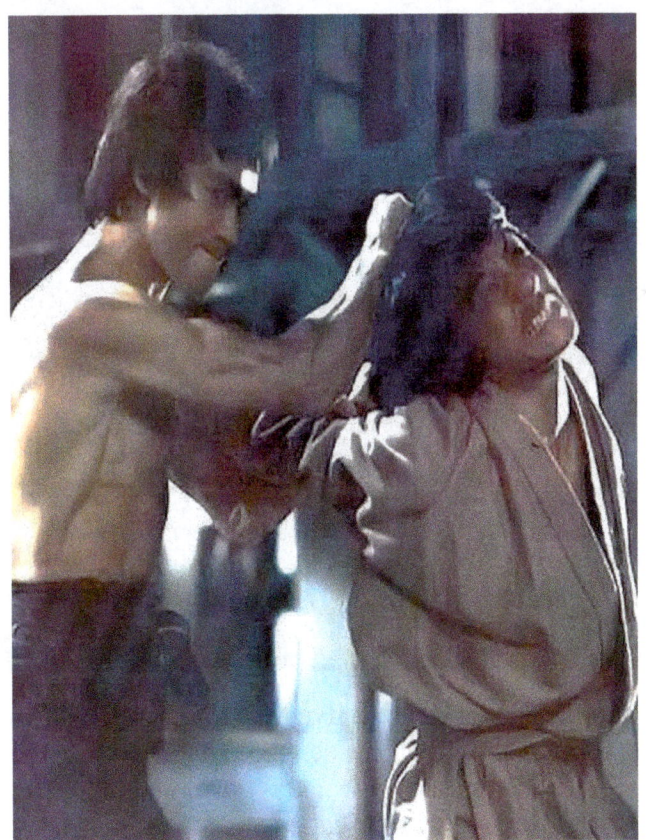

Bruce vs. Jackie Chan

Furthermore, Bruce Lee relentlessly trained hundreds of our Special Forces (Green Beret) during the Viet Nam War! I've spoken to them and they are eternally grateful for learning secrets that are not even taught today by Bruce's original students who later became JKD instructors themselves.

Although born in San Francisco but lived in Hong Kong before returning to the U.S. to claim American citizenship, Bruce Lee joined the military but was not drafted. Ironically, he failed the medical for myopia; it was attributed to him saying , "I must be the fittest man ever to fail the military medical exam."

Kato, a name held in high esteem. Thanks, James Harness!

SUPPLANTING JAMES

Early on in the second season, Dave Turin, who was well respected by everyone, became Todd's right hand man supplanting James Harness as the technical expert. Thinking that he may be on the way out, James confided in me while we were on the trek up to Alaska and the Yukon, that he submitted his list of recommendations for Todd to improve overall mining operations. It was either rejected or neglected purposely. Todd relied less on James for short and long-term consultation. James said to me, "I'm going to bring my lady friend up as a witness."

James told me that he needed someone to corroborate and document what transpired on the show. He was misused as an adviser and consultant. James felt his personal well-being was at risk. The injuries that resulted from a rear-ended automobile crash severely impacted his life. In other words, he clearly and emphatically said, "I was hired to be a consultant only, advising others on how to do the actual work."

This was clearly shown as it unfolded during season one. James' body literally shut down on more than one occasion. Off-season, James underwent a medical procedure to ameliorate his vertebrae problems. Only the symptoms were addressed. There was no cure for the root problem. Many in the audience empathized with James' predicament and felt that he was unduly abused by the demands placed on him physically. Instead of addressing the many symptoms (which included unrelenting electrical pain that shot down his legs and muscle spasms that emanated from his lower back vertebrae), they needed to find a way to reconnect the disjointed, crushed spinal vertebrae and reconstruct the spinal cord which would break the cycle of pain for longer than a few days. I asked James whether or not he would consider Stanford Medical Center for a credible diagnosis leading to an actual prognosis. He said, "I'll give it a shot."

Remember this: James had to make a decision of choosing to stay with the team in Alaska or to return home to visit his dying mother. I hope sharing this clears some of the air and sheds more light of that episodic period in James' tenure as the "go to man."

GIRLFRIEND

Harness abandoned work to spend time with his girlfriend/fiancé who came to visit him. That was the situation portrayed seen in the show. James Harness tells Kato the real reasons for having her in the Yukon.

According to James he said that when he couldn't work he needed her to corroborate his story. He also wanted her to support his testimony of being used as a laborer instead of an adviser (as contracted with Todd). During the first season, James had to spend hours in the camper shell resting because of his back pain and other illnesses.

Additionally, she could help him physically. A mere shift of the leg or a simple slight twist in his hips could send electrical shocks throughout his lower extremities that could last anywhere for minutes to several hours, which was a very painful and paralyzing experience. Jack could attest to this since he had off-season back surgery to alleviate severe back pain.

PAROLE EVIDENCE

I discussed a plethora of issues with Todd inside his RV during and after each day of traveling and shooting in Alaska and the Yukon. I described how individuals in the corporate world, the military, and all walks of life were successful. Todd listened quite gingerly and attentively and I always (99%) wrote them down - parole evidence. These recommendations and advice were gladly received; I told him I didn't want them forgotten. At one point, I made a list of recommendations to improve upon the operation of his mining/TV mission. As an (systems) analyst, it was incumbent for me to advise him to delegate some of his more mundane duties to someone else and focus on the primary decision-making responsibilities. The following examples are just a few of our discussions reduced under parole evidence:

TO   : T. Hoffman
FROM   : R. Chin
SUBJECT : Organization=Productivity=More Time
DATE   : 20 May 2011

On-going objective observation suggest the following recommendations for systems organization; improved productivity and more time for creativity (your forte).

-- 2nd cellphone exclusive for inner circle (generally under 3) e.g. CEO, COO

-- Select individual to head all corporate and communication appointments and schedules

-- All discussions be reduced to writing on one (1) page [same as General and President Eisenhower]

-- Select and delegate limited authority to screen all business opportunities

-- Eliminate personal and corporate communication via e-mail, face book, internet and delegate responsibility to second tier individual/circle

-- Final decisions by Messr. Hoffman through one (1) page summary recommendation(s) followed by optional/mandatory personal meetings arranged by appointment secretary

TO   : T. Hoffman
From   : R. Chin
SUBJECT: Cable Channel Acquisition
DATE   : 25 May 2011

Per conversation this morning regarding a cable TV channel acquisition as the vehicle to convey and exploit Messr. Hoffman's television programming and platform, it was recommended to initiate an immediate search. Upon successful completion of due diligence, including viewership numbers, sponsorships, target market, an underperforming channel would be selected as the least expensive to acquire.

HAINES, ALASKA

In preparation of satisfying the mining regulations of the U.S Department of Labor Mine Safety and Health Administration (MSHA) under Public Law 91-173, everyone was required to receive classroom instruction and pass a written examination in order to receive their certificate of training. On the morning of May 8, 2011, we were professionally and thoroughly instructed (despite objections at the outset from one attendee that the instruction would be redundant) at a classroom in the local high school: the rudiments of the work environment, hazard recognition, emergency medical procedures, health and safety standards and tasks assigned, self-rescue and respiratory devices, transport and communication systems, evacuation, cleanup, and so forth. As far as I know, everyone passed (I missed one question because I misconstrued the instructor's semantics of a mining definition when I asked him - I never had any mining instruction prior to this).

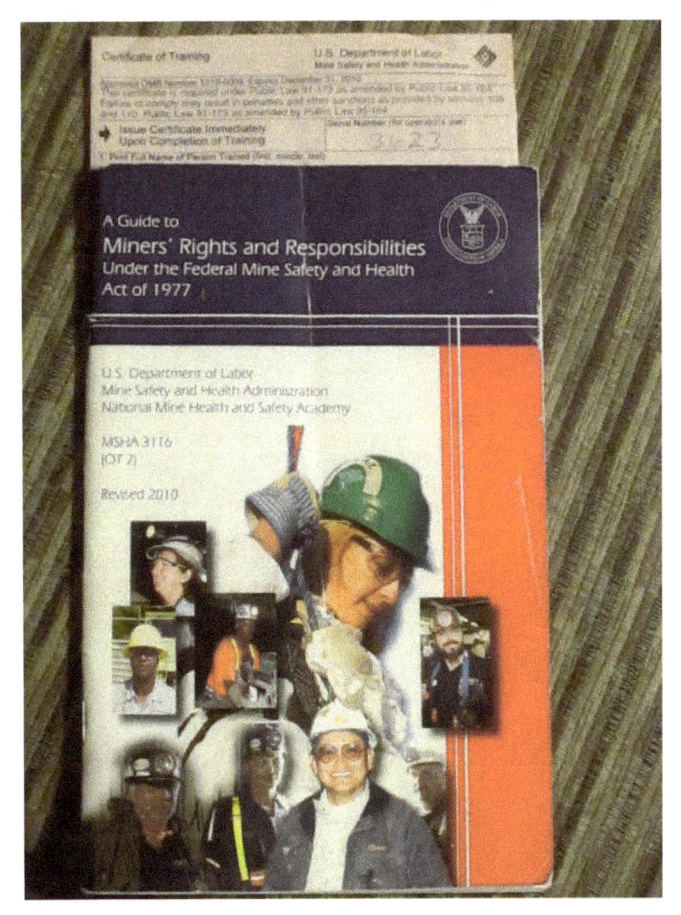

CROSS-MARKETING AGREEMENT

This Cross-marketing Agreement (this "Agreement"), made and entered into on this ___ day of _____, 2011 (the "Effective Date"), is by and between Noble Bullion, Inc. ("Noble") and G3 Promotions, LLC ("G3").

WHEREAS, Noble is a company that is in the business of dealing in precious metals, and intends to develop business activities in precious metal mining, mining clubs, prospecting travel and equipment, prospecting education, real estate promotion of patented and leased land or claims, and other related activities in and around the mining, prospecting, and bullion investment sector.

WHEREAS, G3 is the business agent for Jerusalem Mining, LLC ("Jerusalem"), and is involved in distribution, marketing, and exploitation of the reality television series titled "Gold Rush Alaska" (the "Series"); and

WHEREAS, Noble, and G3 (with Jerusalem) desire to enter into an independent contractor arrangement by which Noble can take advantage of marketing opportunities afforded by consultation with G3, and participation in the Series, and G3 can take advantage of Noble's expertise, access to markets for its products and business activities and opportunities.

NOW, THEREFORE, in consideration for the premises and promises contained herein, and for other good and valuable consideration, the receipt and sufficiency of which is hereby acknowledged, Noble and G3, intending to be legally bound, hereby agree as follows:

1. Term. Unless earlier terminated in accordance with the terms and conditions of this Agreement, this Agreement shall be and remain in effect for the period beginning on the Effective Date and ending on June 31, 2016 (the "Term"). Within six (6) months prior to the expiration of the Term, Noble may elect to negotiate in good faith with G3 on an exclusive basis for a period of six (6) weeks regarding an extension of the Term, unless Noble agrees otherwise.

2. Noble's Obligations. Noble shall perform as follows during the Term:

a. Initial Marketing Loan Commitment. Noble will loan G3 a maximum of $250,000.00, the loan to be evidenced by promissory notes in the form attached as Exhibit "A" hereto, and said promissory note shall be secured by the collateral described in, and subject to, a security agreement in the form attached hereto as "Exhibit B" hereto.

b. Initial Year Compensation. Upon satisfactory performance by G3 of its obligations hereunder and the satisfaction of the conditions precedent for the contingent compensation expressed in paragraph 2c. below, or, alternatively at Noble's discretion in the event the conditions precedent are not satisfied, Noble will pay G3 $250,000.00, for the 2011 production of the Series, or, alternatively at Noble's discretion will forgive the payment obligations of the Promissory Note.

c. Contingent Compensation. In further consideration for the performance of G3's obligations under this Agreement, and the marketing opportunities afforded Noble, the following contingent compensation will be paid to G3, subject to the following conditions

1

IN WITNESS WHEREOF, Noble and G3 have executed this Agreement on, and this Agreement shall be deemed effective as of, the Effective Date.

NOBLE BUILLION, INC.   **G3 PROMOTIONS, LLC**

By: _____   By: _____

Print Name: _____   Print Name: _____

Title: _____   Title: _____

GUARANTY

This Guaranty (this "Guaranty") is made part of, and is hereby incorporated by reference into, the above Agreement for all purposes. For good and valuable consideration, the receipt and sufficiency of which is hereby acknowledged, Jerusalem Mining, LLC ("Guarantor"), by its signature below and as of the Effective Date, does hereby guaranty to Noble the timely performance of each and every obligation of G3 under this Agreement. This Guaranty is made for the benefit of Noble and its affiliates, successors, and assigns, and is binding on Guarantor and its affiliates, successors, and assigns.

                              GUARANTOR: Jerusalem Mining, LLC

                              By: _____
                              Print Name: _____
                              Title: _____

ACKNOWLEDGED AND AGREED TO BY:

Noble Bullion, Inc.   G3 Promotions, LLC

By: _____   By: _____
Print Name: _____   Print Name: _____
Title: _____   Title: _____

A week and a half later while having dinner in a Haines restaurant, Todd received a written bilateral contract on his electronic device from the legal representatives of Nobile Bullion, Inc. It was regarding a contractual agreement between the two parties. He asked me to review it and I recommended recision on the grounds of exposure to liability personally and severally from resulting association with the other party. As a result, Todd/RAW had to backtrack the storyline by filming (a) new episode(s) disassociating his relationship with the aforementioned without reproof.

```
TO      : T. Hoffman
FROM    : R. Chin
SUBJECT : Noble Bullion
DATE    : 20 May 2011

Per conversation two days ago regarding recission of relationship
with Noble Bullion (TV and monetary consideration), please be
advised that legal and regulatory consequences may seriously
jeopardize the operation, filming, worldwide exploitation of
Gold Rush be made in accordance with the undersigned below, sic
Messr. T. Hoffman, et al. Further, personal, family, corporate
assets, goodwill and any and all future enterprises may be sub-
ject to legal, judicial and regulatory review and/or attachment.
In view of the foregoing, it is recommended that simple dis-
claimer is insufficient to avoid personal due diligence and
responsibility on behalf of television and publishing media
(interstate commerce and banking).
```

PROVOST MARSHAL

Provost Marshal, charged with police functions working with the commander, was one of the hats I wore on this trip. Instead of James being the watchdog for the camp as he was in the first season (while Todd and the others left the grounds of Porcupine Creek for dinner or whatever reason - shopping, re-supplying, washing clothes, etc.), I became the unofficial watchdog, thereby alleviating James some physical stress and giving him more quality sleep. Since I didn't have to endure the daily grind of operating heavy machinery, driving loaders, maneuvering equipment, making repairs and servicing vehicles, there was no need for me to be concerned with my physical well-being during the day, except for watching for Todd's back at public functions in Haines and in Dawson City.

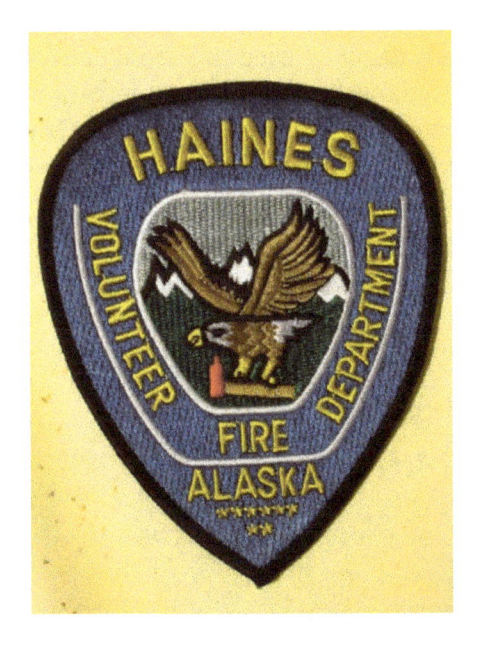

Haines Fire Dept.   Haines Police Dept.

The following are some examples in this role.
Incidents:

During the ride with James, the caravan stopped for the night at a Walmart parking lot in lower British Columbia. Canadian Carl's was a few steps away so I stayed behind while they ate. I didn't want to be a burden to anyone and wanted to contribute in whatever way I can. I watched or stood guard whenever the guys ate out or when they went swimming in a hot spring/pool to keep onlookers from becoming souvenir collectors. At night, the guys slept while I stayed outside walking guard. An incident occurred when some individuals in a pickup attempted to take something from the back of one of our trucks. When I approached them, they scampered like cockroaches when the kitchen lights flicked on. Another incident of note took place when we were in the Gold Rush RV park in Dawson City (that's their real name - how's that for coincidence). About an hour before sunrise (ambush hour), a guy was scouring the back of the pickups. When he got to Thurber's RV, I got out and ordered him to freeze; I chased after him to no avail. At least nothing was taken from our group.

    I saw someone approaching our RV while staying up one night. It wasn't a local tenant since he made a double bee-line for Jack's RV. I grabbed Jack's 12 gauge, racked a round (woke Blue up in the process) and pointed it at his head as soon as he opened both the screen and door. I ordered him to get out of the RV and drop to the ground. I called the RCMP (Royal Canadian Mounted Police) who arrived shortly thereafter. They cuffed the intruder and took him away in their unit without further incident. A report was made when they interviewed me later at Wayne Fisher's grounds. I tried to keep it at a low profile but rumors were flying in from RAW and/or Discovery that a kidnapping attempt was made on one of the Gold Rush members. I learned of it that morning when Dave Turin told me he thought he heard loud voices and yelling between his and Jack's RV. I said, "I didn't hear nothing."

BEAR HUNT

While in Alaska, we ate at the 33 Mile Roadhouse Restaurant - it had great food and great customers.

I used the restaurant's restroom as my daily wash facility. A lot of locals came here to see us. A helipad and fuel station next to the restaurant brought even more customers. Why did I bring this up? This was my launching point to hunt for bears. Yes, I had a hunting license and bear permits. At the time, I was the only member of Todd's group who had successfully hunted bear on more than one occasion. Very early in the hunting season, I went tracking across the area. When I returned the next day, the workers in the restaurant reported seeing bears not far from them. I borrowed Jack's shotgun and carried a pocketful of double 00 buckshot rounds, slugs and a knife, and some day-old salmon (bait) to take on the hunt.

Further assumption that we were heading into Canada and not staying in Alaska was the fact that no one was allowed to bring pistols with him since they are banned there. As a point of reference during the first season, Todd and the others had the .50 caliber Magnum Research elephant gun semi-auto pistols with them.

After I was gone for a couple of days and returned empty handed, RAW and Todd's group wondered whether Alaskan grizzly bears enjoyed eating Chinese take-out.

JIM DORSEY

While at Porcupine Creek, I was told by a number of guys that Jim Dorsey, one of the original cast members who left abruptly before the first season's last episode, wanted to be in front of the camera as much as possible. The same guys stated that the reason for more questionable, erratic on-screen behavior was possibly, "Dorsey's temporary cessation of taking his normal prescription(s)". Since there was no love lost for him, they razed the wooden structure at the mine site that he used to live in.

FLAG RAISING

While filming a flag raising "ceremony" at Porcupine Creek, I gave very specific instructions which Jim Thurber (unintentionally) didn't follow. Tim Dalby, RAW's best cameraman, apologized to me thinking that formalities may not have been observed on such a solemn occasion and explained that they meant no disrespect. All of the members of Gold Rush, at least the ones that I've been so fortunate to be associated with, agreed with me that RAW's camera people, sound technicians, support staff, directors and supervisors were truly professional and conducted themselves in the same way off-screen.

I don't know whether it was true or not; as a postscript, someone later told me that they shot my reaction from a distance and wanted it on the show.

FOREHAND KNOWLEDGE

When our caravan group returned to their original Alaskan gold site, Todd already knew that they were going to the Yukon. Excuses were made that the water level in the river was too low for mining purposes. In reality, the man who "sold" them the idea of a rich gold reserve on the Porcupine Creek property "lied" according to Todd, who confided in me. The draining of the glory hole "lake" and other incidents proved nothing more than a ruse to fill in empty plot holes early in the second season. Unless there were really exciting shots and dramatics to be made, the show faced a roadblock. Whether Discovery advised Todd or not about the need for more action sequences, the senior management inserted Dakota Fred and then Parker as competing characters of Gold Rush - first in supporting roles, then permanent ones.

It was easy to see Todd lose grip of the show by letting it slip through his fingers. Money would be the only compensation he could get for losing editing control.

LOSING CONTROL

Todd gave birth to Gold Rush and Discovery took it away from him. Discovery added other characters that had their own mining operations. First was Dakota Fred's, then young Parker's (in physical age, certainly not in mental and physical experience). Similar shows like Bering Sea Gold appeared. I found out about that particular show while it was still on the drawing board; I couldn't notify Todd about it since he kept changing his cell phone number. There are all kinds of gold shows, prospecting shows and even Alaskan shows now. I'm sure the grandeur of Todd's initial success had been diminished and it may even have gotten under his crawl (humanly speaking of course). If I know Todd though, I'm sure he'll rise above it all and look up.

"N" WORD

One evening in Todd's RV, there was casual talk. Todd asked Kato about "C_____" emphasizing higher education in their culture. I said, "What!" Everyone looked at his reddening face, much like Obama's was when he was in Hawaii on one of his latest holiday junket when he described the military audience's appearance as Santa's fatigues instead of their distinctive, professional BDU's. You could almost hear a pin drop when Obama finally broke the deafening silence by going into repair mode, stuttering for words.

Todd similarly apologized but was sincerely miffed in using that language. I said, "You wouldn't use the "N" word to an African American?" Todd said, "Of course not." To turn this embarrassing situation around, I cited the incident that occurred when I accompanied decorated Korean War hero Colonel Ralph Hodge, a member of my board of directors who vied for the permanent berthing of the U.S.S. Missouri (on-board signing of Imperial Japan's surrender in WW2) in San Francisco (The Mighty Mo went to Pearl Harbor), to an event headlined by General Colin Powell, then Secretary of State and America's would be first Black president, had he accepted Governor Bush's offer as Vice President in 2000. As a former protégé of General Powell, Colonel Hodge was instantly recognized when General Powell stood up and grabbed his right hand with both of his and they each exchanged more than a few pleasantries. They talked soldier to soldier. Very similarly, as Chairman of the Joint Chiefs of Staff under two presidents, General Powell used that same "C_____" word not knowing that it was improper and inappropriate; he apologized as well.

I told Todd, "You're in good company!" As an addendum to conclude this story, General Powell personally wrote back to thank me (classy man, that General).

JAMES' SECRET

Todd tells me that "James' back condition is not as serious as you might think." Todd's underestimation or deliberate oversight of James Harness' back problem is an issue that should be addressed.

James is not a crybaby in any sense of the word. Even after James' back condition worsened during Gold Rush's maiden season, he chose not to talk about his health and just withheld as much detail as possible. Rather than divulge the actual condition of his back and overall health, I pressed him for more information during our trek to and through Alaska and Canada. Since I was wearing the "hat" of a medic as well as being enclosed in a vehicle for thousands of miles together, you might say that James was my captive audience.

If Todd knew of James' real condition, would this be a wanton act of malfeasance or abuse or even endangering his welfare? I dare say that James' condition bordered the side of critical to dangerous. After consulting with the top medical specialists of major universities (which included department heads), they agreed that James' condition, the result of an automobile rear-end collision, left him in an appalling state. He should not have ventured out traveling by car or truck for long distances, let alone perform heavy equipment repair and the like. I accompanied James' visits to specialists in order to seek "simple" pain relief; however, the treatments offered only temporary relief. The auto accident, in addition injured his shoulder and limbs, pretty much left his spinal column mangled and disjointed. To reiterate, there was no continuous, connected spine with discs separating the vertebrae. Some discs disintegrated to the point where vertebrae was grinding on vertebrae. The mere thought of just arthritic (bone on bone) pain pales to insignificance when compared with vertebrae on vertebrae connected to the entire central nervous system!

In an almost surreal-like state as he was driving on a really long stretch, James tells me that, "If I ever get permanently fixed (surgically), I kind of like to use my truck for slow and large equipment escorting."

NAPOLEONIC COMPLEX

I failed to understand why Todd "made" us watch the same movie over and over again in his RV at night. Perhaps it was the good food, snacks and refreshments that he generously offered that made us his captive audience.

I brought up many DVDs with me, including several of Steve McQueen's. One show that Todd particularly enjoyed was McQueen's inaugural television series "Wanted Dead or Alive". I mentioned that Steve McQueen was raised in Boy's Town, since he had no father, didn't like to read a lot and was a streetwise kid. Afterwards, we discussed some trivia of the stars. In McQueen's case, I told them that he was remembered for being a very generous man, not only with his time but with his money. For example, when San Francisco mayor Joseph Alioto gave almost carte blanche to the production of "Bullitt", McQueen donated his funds for the construction of a swimming pool in the Bay View District of the City.

The filming of Irwin Allen's catastrophe movie "The Towering Inferno" took place across the street from my office. I saw Fred Astaire dancing up and down the Tower's stairs, O.J. Simpson and Paul Newman were walking into the (Bank of America HQ) building dressed in their costume wardrobe and Steve McQueen was in his battalion chief's fireman's geared uniform. Most recently, I learned from one of his friends that McQueen consistently gave many charitable gifts and supported many causes without publicity, a trait seldom seen today. Even rarer still, that a tough guy like John Wayne or McQueen, be emulated as a man's man who is humble and has a heart. I apologize to have to go off on a tangent but there are similarities that you can draw between them and Todd (to be explained later).

Todd watched "Napoleon Dynamite" over and over again (I couldn't watch it after the second viewing). Despite a paltry production budget, the movie grossed over nine figures! Relatively recently, Fox attempted and failed to air a full season the animated version of "Napoleon Dynamite" on prime time Sunday evening. To date, I haven't the foggiest idea why he repeatedly watches it (perhaps, the sight and sound of theatrical revenue?) except maybe he has a complex.

SETTING AN EXAMPLE

Jack and I talked for hours about military life. Whether we talked at restaurants or in his RV, we had a special camaraderie that only military people can have. No matter what subject or experience we shared, it was great fellowship. While conversing with him about his Army career, I was reminded of three men who made an indelible impression on me and they will always be my life's example.

Col. Ralph Hodge, a fellow board member on various non-profit organizations that I have had the pleasure of working with, served with distinction during the Korean War. He had just received his Purple Heart and other decorations the Pentagon failed to initially deliver. (Hodge first introduced me to then Chairman of the Joint Chiefs of Staff, Gen. Colin Powell).

Lt. Col. Charles Robinson was a Filipino Scout who helped lead the Philippine Resistance that saved thousands of American soldiers' lives.

> "These inadequately armed patriots have fought the enemy for more than two years. Their names and deeds shall ever be enshrined in the hearts of our two peoples",
>
> General Douglas MacArthur.

In the midst of rescuing Americans and other Allies, Robinson was captured by the Japanese. He escaped and was recaptured again. While imprisoned, Robinson became bitter when he was left behind and not rescued like the others. When the Korean War erupted, he volunteered again and served with distinction. When Robinson met the Lord, bitterness left him and he became the Army chaplain for HQ's staff.

Col. George Yanehiro, born in the U.S., imprisoned with his family after the sneak attack on Pearl Harbor, joined the Army's 442nd and served in Europe, the highest decorated combat unit in WW2. He served with distinction and later became a California Superior Court judge. I often ask myself, "How can anyone do what he did in WW2 after the way they treated his family and friends so despicably?" One day, I gathered enough courage, walked over and raised my salute to him and asked the Colonel, "What were you thinking of when you and your battalion were fighting in all of those campaigns when our government stateside imprisoned and spat on you and your family?"

LTC Robinson Col. Yanehiro

After a moment that seemed like minutes, he returned my salute; I then lowered mine. Yanehiro breaks a tortuous smile and did not utter a word. I knew his WW2 service were the darkest hours of his life and that he relives it every day.

When President Reagan was honoring CMH recipients at the White House, he said, "Where do we get such men?"

Since 9-11, I always stop non-coms in uniform in airports overseas and offer a few words of encouragement, a meal (and/or a little money), and a prayer of gratitude before they arrive for or return to duty. It is hoped that others would join me in sharing the same sentiment - that we stand firmly behind them unconditionally.

CENSORSHIP

According to Todd and others, there was constant "censoring" of words that were never used by the original cast members in seasons one and two. Although there was legitimate censoring of the other group members in season two - Dakota Fred and Parker - excessive "bleeps" were deliberately inserted to give the impression of so called "heightened interest." During my stay in season two, I did not hear any of Todd's original cast members use obscene language or expletives on or off filming, except for one instance. Furthermore, Todd was concerned with Discovery's editing when his crew prayed.

BAD MOUTHING

It's bad enough to speak negatively about your spouse. But to do it publicly in front of everyone in Dave's RV during breakfast and Bible study is another story. Todd stated that he didn't trust his wife with a checking account. (Frankly, I don't even trust myself with a checking account. If I did, I wouldn't be writing this book!) We don't know what prompted Todd to make that remark, but he did tell me that he left his home church when his wife initiated an erroneous rumor falsely circulated by that pastor's wife.

By the way, I share with Todd's decision in bringing Dave up permanently for the second season. Preparing early every morning with not just a hot breakfast for Todd's team and guest(s), Dave studied and offered spiritual breakfast, the most important sustenance of the day. Dave's skills, expertise and leadership definitely provided esprit de corps and made a difference. Mark one up for Todd's decisiveness here.

While spending time at the Sandy Airport, Todd took me around to eat (Toll's, Outback Steakhouse...) and went to church service. I don't mind saying this - Todd humbles himself before God, even to the point of asking for His help on his knees while we attended a Sunday morning service. Todd got his priorities right.

DESTINATION KLONDIKE

After a "short" drive from Haines, Alaska and stopped at the Canadian border for verification and compliance, the caravan continued onward for hours. Unless they wanted to publicly divulge, I was unaware if anyone else aside from Todd (and Jack) knew where we were headed. We trekked our way until we finally reached the far end of town and found ourselves in Dawson City.

Herein is a brief synopsis:

Dawson City, Yukon is the heart of the world-famous Klondike Gold Rush. On August 17, 1896, three "Sourdoughs", George Carmack, Dawson Charlie and Skookum Jim found gold on Rabbit Creek (now Bonanza Creek), a tributary of the Klondike River. Another account puts Mrs. Carmack making the discovery while she was washing George's clothes off another Klondike stream. By the way, the semantics of the word Klondike came from the Northwest Native American Indian word "ThronDiuck" = "hammer water"=KLON-DIKE with a slur of the tongue. Word of this find quickly spread to about a thousand prospectors, miners, Northwest Mounted Police, missionaries and others who called the Yukon home at the time. Settlements were quickly abandoned as a rush to stake the best ground commenced. Two of these residents were Joe Ladue and Arthur Harper, who had traded in the Yukon for years. They were quick to purchase, stake and establish the town site of Dawson (named for Canadian geologist George Mercer Dawson) at the confluence of the Yukon and Klondike Rivers, about 12 miles from Discovery Claim.

News reached the outside world in July of 1897 when the steamships Excelsior and Portland reached San Francisco and Seattle respectively, with the successful miners from the previous season carrying the infamous "Ton of Gold." News spread like wildfire of a land where "nuggets could be picked off the creek floor" to a recession suffering world and caused an unprecedented stampede of an estimated 100,000 people to set out to the Klondike. They followed treacherous routes that involved uncharted landscapes, snow-choked mountain passes and freezing rivers to stake their claim to fortune in the Klondike. Most would need to travel over 3,000 land miles to get to Dawson City.

In 1898, Dawson City quickly grew as 30,000 pick-and-shovel miners, prospectors, storekeepers, bankers, saloon keepers, gamblers, prostitutes and adventure seekers took over the town site. Most arrived to discover the good ground had been staked. Many left but others stayed and made fortunes through other endeavors. From 1896-1899, $29 million in gold was mined around Dawson City. In today's dollars that would be (using rule of 72) in excess of $400 million.

As the "Paris of the North" and the largest city west of Winnipeg and north of Seattle, Dawson City thrived with millionaires roaming the streets seeking ways to spend their riches on the best food, drink and clothing at a high cost. Dance and gambling halls, bars, brothels, restaurants and supply stores all made fortunes "mining the miners."

Dawson City continued to thrive until gold was found on the beaches of Nome, Alaska in 1899. Many of the same people who came seeking fortunes in the Klondike left Dawson in a new gold rush. As in every GOLD RUSH, most participants found no gold at all. Notwithstanding, we're no exception and we come with great anticipation.

Upon arrival at Dawson City's Gold Rush (RV) Campground, I partook of the delightful cuisine that James created with the beef that he brought up in a chest freezer.

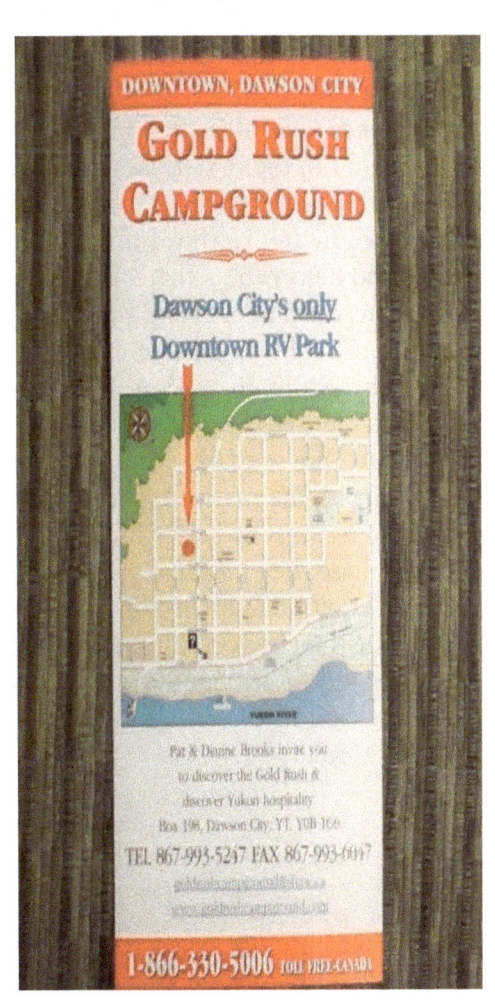

James had the foresight of knowing what was in store for us. We all found out shortly thereafter that the cost of eating out was very prohibitive. Some examples: a simple breakfast of eggs, hash browns and toast cost approximately 10 Canadian dollars ($13 U.S.) or a hamburger at Sourdough Joe's for about 18 Canadian dollars ($21 U.S.). Don't forget the tip. Imagine the cost of dinner! By Territorial edict, Dawson City was prohibited in constructing commercial-eating franchises along the likes of Wendy's/McDonald's/Carl's Jr. Fortunately for us, the benevolence of RAW and their crew members enabled us to enjoy delicious gourmet sandwiches that were provided to them. As part of Todd's bargaining power, a midday lunch became a welcomed standard for all of us. I will always remember the generosity of the Fishers. Mrs. Fisher labored early in the morning to prepare a scrumptious dinner for everyone (cast & crew) that rivaled those of the French Laundry in Northern California (voted #1 restaurant in the world by Michelin in 2005 & 2006). I reciprocated by taking the Fishers to their favorite restaurant in Dawson City.

James took measures to be more self-reliant instead of riding along with someone else as he did in the first season. Rather than lose his personal and expensive Snap-On Tools that he had to use in Alaska (which were borrowed or lost) he supplanted that problem by introducing Harbor Freight to me before we left Sandy. We loaded up on all kinds of hand and heavy tools that were deemed necessary, thus safeguarding his expensive tools for his custom cars and bikes.

James told me that he needed to pace himself because he knew how few miles he had left physically. In order to "document" his condition and the demands placed on him by Todd, supposedly as an adviser and not as an everyday laborer, James invited his lady-friend up to Dawson City. Yes, there was time for fellowship, but not in the same line as compared with the married men who brought their wives and other family members with them. Two reasons in James thinking. First, he needed to pace himself physically and needed to hide the ongoing spasms in his back that could trigger anytime, especially under heavy, strenuous physical demands. Secondly, James told me that in the first season of Gold Rush he stayed behind watching for outside intruders. He guarded the RVs and everything else in the camp against unwanted thrill seekers riding enduros through and around the camp.

"BULLITT"

In the epic scene where Bullitt's (Steve McQueen's) Mustang chased a Charger up and down the hilly streets of San Francisco, it depicts the authority in the Ford versus the criminal in the Dodge. The producer of this film did not want to use only Fords on the movie set and wanted something like an ominous shark by using a black Dodge Charger. James and I were watching Bullitt when we had dinner in his camper one evening. Little did we know that a few days later, we were going to witness the tables turned around, albeit 40 plus years later.

Miles before pulling into the mine site, our caravan pulled stakes leaving the tranquility of Dawson City. Chris was in the process of towing his "new"ly acquired RV up a 20-degree incline dirt road; all of a sudden, it began to struggle and slip - no torque. Finally, his F350 truck and trailer just stopped. While everyone was scratching their head trying to figure put what to do, Jack, with his ole Army professional experience, ordered everyone to stand down as he aligned his Dodge truck in front of Chris' Ford and hooked it with chains. Everyone shook their heads and thought that Chris needed a dozer or a F550 tow truck to pull both the truck and RV trailer out of the rut and into the base camp.

As Jack moved his Dodge forward taking the slack out of the tow, he began to crack a smile at me, a widening smile at RAW and other crew members and with white teeth grinning ear to ear (aka Lewis Carroll's Cheshire Cat) he looked at Chris (who was inside his cab who was hoping to steer), as he put his Dodge truck into four-wheel drive. Some brown dirt, dust and pebbles begin to fly as the wheels spun - Chris' eyes began to pop out as all the wheels were moving. To everyone's amazement, we all began to clap our hands and applauded Jack coming to the rescue, again. All during this "episode", Kato recorded all the action with his side-holstered Canon camcorder. Jack rolled his eyes as suggestions were made to re-enact this incident so that RAW could shoot it for the show. Sometime later, the idea of having a Ford pickup and RV being towed by a Dodge truck gained momentum as an indirect product placement. We all smiled as we envisioned Chrysler Corporation's executives drooling in anticipation of a marketing campaign. I won't name names but a suggestion was made by one of our guys for Ford would have to pay a fee for not having Gold Rush air that incident.

Chris or James diagnosed the seizure to be a tranny (transmission) problem that

Chris traced to RAW when they "borrowed" his truck earlier. When he confronted those responsible, they pretty much hung their heads low and plead innocence like a kid caught with his hand stuck in the cookie jar. As usual, Chris, like Jack, also exemplified professionalism by not pursuing it further. Chris sucked up the $4,000-plus transmission overhaul/replacement cost with a shrug of his shoulders and just smiled.

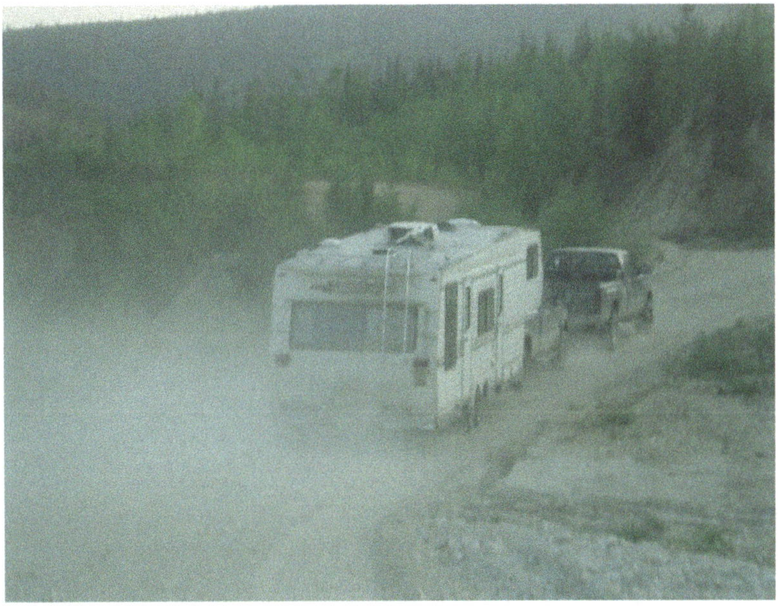

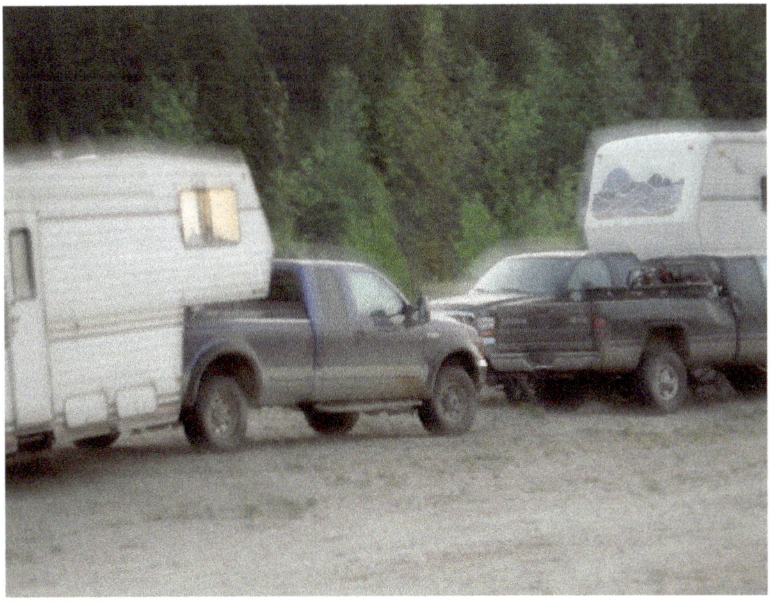

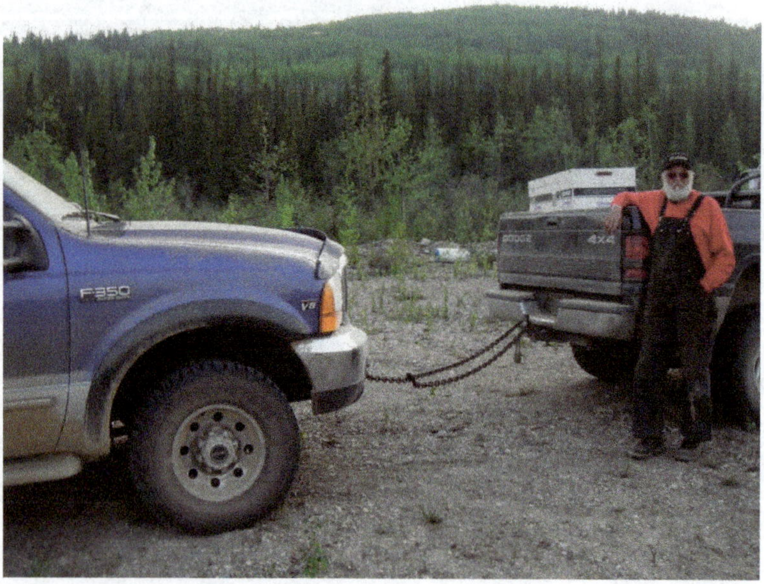
F350
V8
DODGE
4X4

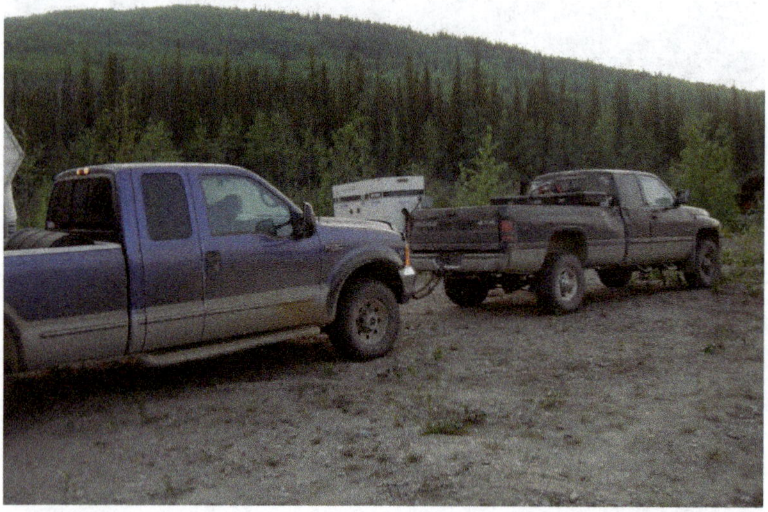

Notch another mark on Jack's shotgun (for Dodge)

WOUNDED WARRIORS

    Kato accompanied Chris and Jack to Alaska for a bear hunt with members of the Wounded Warrior Foundation. With their invitation, we flew with the pilot. There was no room for RAW to accompany us to film this expedition – this was another major event that Discovery would have drooled over. Upon arrival in Anchorage, we each stayed in our own hotel rooms and readied ourselves in five hours. The next morning we were escorted onto another flight to the hunting camp. Although everyone knew that the Gold Rush cast members were the celebrities, we made sure that the Wounded Warriors were the true guests of honor.

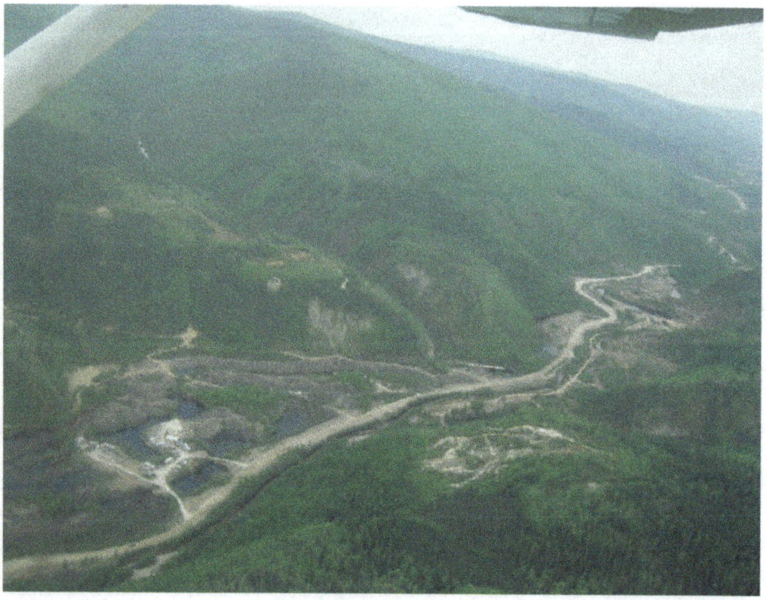

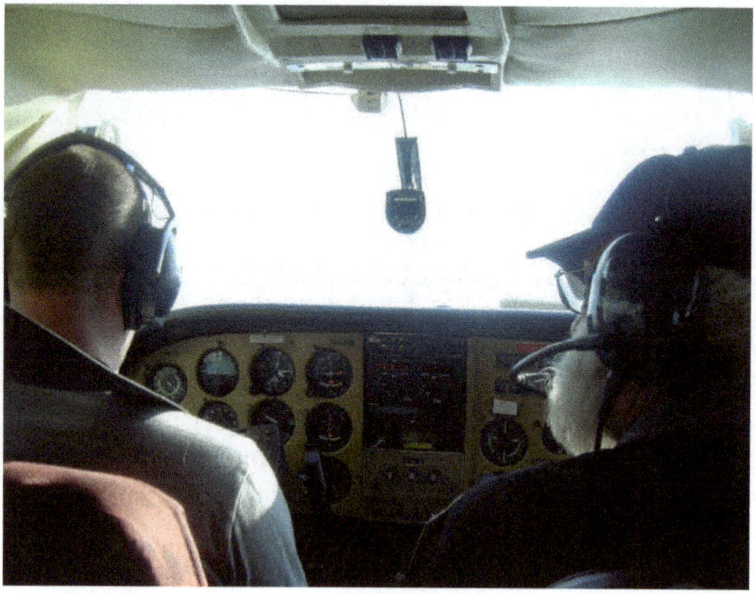

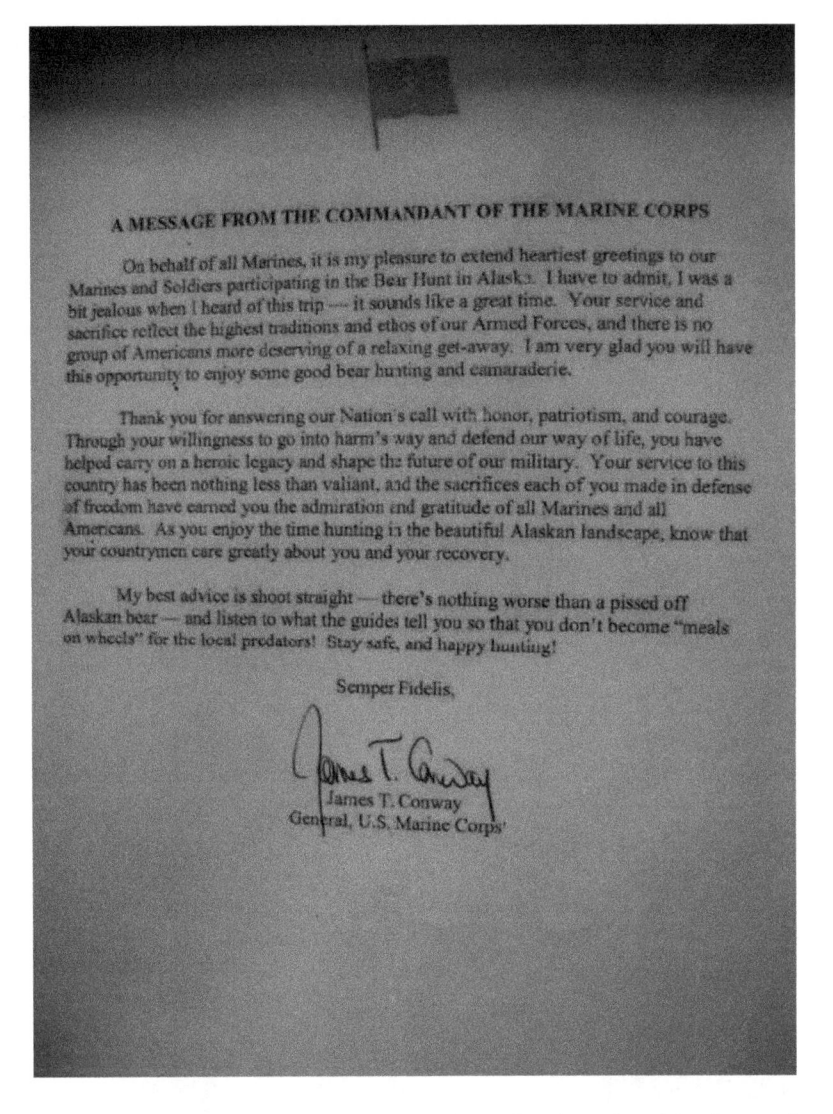

A MESSAGE FROM THE COMMANDANT OF THE MARINE CORPS

On behalf of all Marines, it is my pleasure to extend heartiest greetings to our Marines and Soldiers participating in the Bear Hunt in Alaska. I have to admit, I was a bit jealous when I heard of this trip — it sounds like a great time. Your service and sacrifice reflect the highest traditions and ethos of our Armed Forces, and there is no group of Americans more deserving of a relaxing get-away. I am very glad you will have this opportunity to enjoy some good bear hunting and camaraderie.

Thank you for answering our Nation's call with honor, patriotism, and courage. Through your willingness to go into harm's way and defend our way of life, you have helped carry on a heroic legacy and shape the future of our military. Your service to this country has been nothing less than valiant, and the sacrifices each of you made in defense of freedom have earned you the admiration and gratitude of all Marines and all Americans. As you enjoy the time hunting in the beautiful Alaskan landscape, know that your countrymen care greatly about you and your recovery.

My best advice is shoot straight — there's nothing worse than a pissed off Alaskan bear — and listen to what the guides tell you so that you don't become "meals on wheels" for the local predators! Stay safe, and happy hunting!

Semper Fidelis,

James T. Conway
General, U.S. Marine Corps

I filmed our group with two veterans and professional guides/caretakers who led us to baited sites where the bears would be. Trucks took us to locations behind/near camouflaged areas where we waited and waited. After what seemed to be an hour long wait, a bear was sighted about a half klick away coming from right to left. Patiently, the Army vet pointed the rifle that was provided to him and aimed at the bear. The vet knew the drill. He slowly quieted his breathing and squeezed off a round. Shucks! Low at 3 o'clock. As compensation for not having the scope personally sighted for him, a second round was squeezed off - a miss again but tighter to the left. The dust puff made the bear run off at 11 o'clock. We all started to breathe normally again. What a rush for the shooter and everyone of us! We were all excited. True, he didn't get the bear, but we had really a great time in the camaraderie of the hunt. The hunting guide turned towards me and said, "Your turn". I said, "You're kidding." "Nope." We were all smiles as we were trucked to the next area. This time, I wanted to get off the truck and hike about 50 meters

to the blind just off the road. I waiting for about a half an hour, then I heard something coming towards me. I ducked down to blend in more. Coming around the bend was another truckload of hunters and guides that stopped about 100 meters away. I quickly sounded off my position and they in turned acknowledged my presence. Someone forgot to communicate that this spot was already taken. Oh well, back to the barn – I was thankful that there were no friendly fire issues. We spent great down time with everyone there and bedded down for the night.

      The corporate sponsors and the Wounded Warrior organization really outdid themselves to provide a real turn-key operation for these heroes. Whatever the guests wanted, they cooked to order (free of charge of course). I saw more candy, snacks, soft drinks and juices than a well-stocked PX; all for the taking. This was really a first-class job. My dinner was unbelievable. When I came to Alaska, all I wanted to eat was their fresh native salmon. With a sparkle in his eye, the chef prepared grilled salmon for me, then baked salmon, then fried salmon, then steamed salmon and finally, roasted salmon. I had large portions of each. He really aimed to please! Everyone knows that I am a glutton for punishment, so I brought the salmon leftovers to our cabin and ate some more. Chris and Jack just laughed. Before retiring with a full and content stomach, I told them that I'll be up way before sunrise to go bear hunting alone.

      A couple of hours before the crack of dawn, I holstered a .50 caliber revolver with its belt around my waist (provided by one of the hunting guides) and took some leftover salmon with me. I traversed down a trail and waited for some action. When the mighty Alaskan sun broke the horizon a couple of hours later, I decided to head back to the cabin.

With Jack sleeping and Chris snoring (I meant snoozing) they woke up and realized that I had just returned from the morning hunt. They looked at each other and gasped, "Oh no!"

What if I came across that bear charging at me? Imagine my surprise and disgust at firing an unloaded pistol. They would have returned me back to the Yukon as chow mein! Do you think it was funny, like they did?

In the military, it's a capital offense.

Unlike his usual mild manner, Chris vauntingly jeers,

"Kato, didn't the gun feel lighter to you?"

After exhaling a deep breath and letting my reddened face return to normal, I said to myself, "You gotta love this guy."

FRONT & CENTER

After a photo session with each Wounded Warrior in attendance, we thanked them for their bravery, courage, sacrifice and of course, their service to America in providing freedom for each of us. Even though we first thought that this event was part of a PTSD session, we soon learned that it was far from being one. I thought that some of the attendees were sponsor-coordinators or hunting guides, but they were actually the guest veterans. It was a great program that we all hope will be supported for our brave ones in uniform.

Upon arrival at the Alaskan airport for our departure, there was a solemn ceremony for a Native American who committed suicide. Representatives from the Alaskan State military approached me; I confirmed that there were former members of the American armed services present. With my command voice, unbeknownst to Jack, I said, "Sgt. Hoffman, front and center."

The military members formed a line for ceremonial presentation. Sgt. Jack Hoffman was read an order by the Alaskan state military armed forces representative and a medal with ribbon was placed around his neck. I could see Jack's eyes welling up.

Jack was proud and at the same time humbled when he thought of his service in the Army. Jack did not take off his medal until we landed back in the Yukon. He showed it off to his son and grandsons. I still vividly remember Jack smiling from ear to ear.

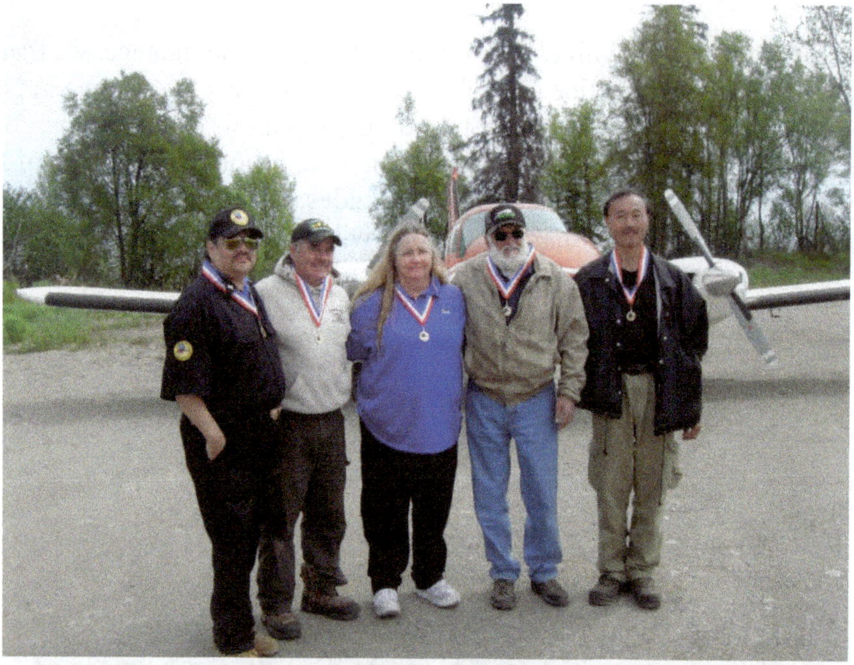

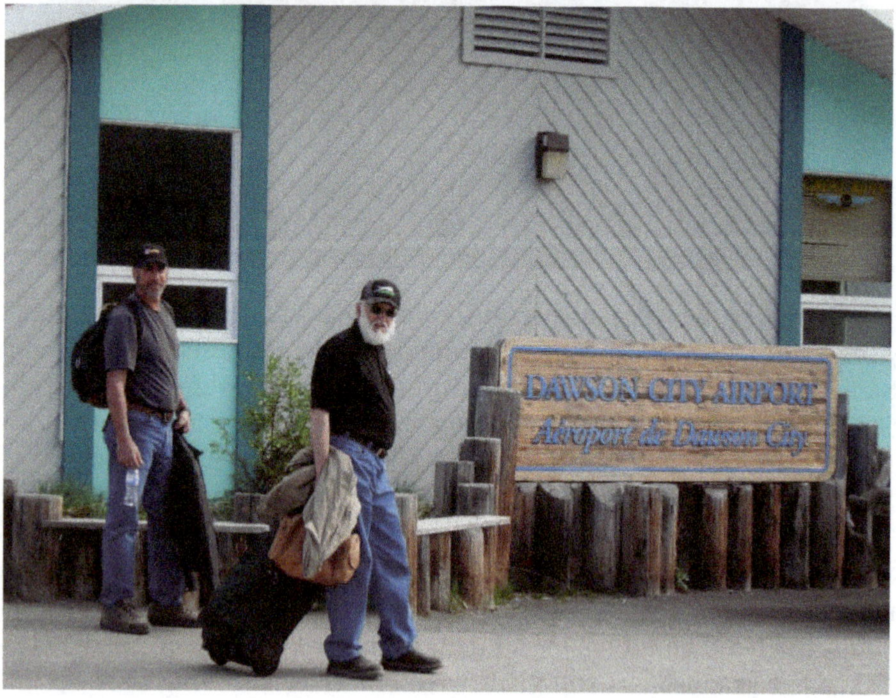
DAWSON CITY AIRPORT
Aéroport de Dawson City

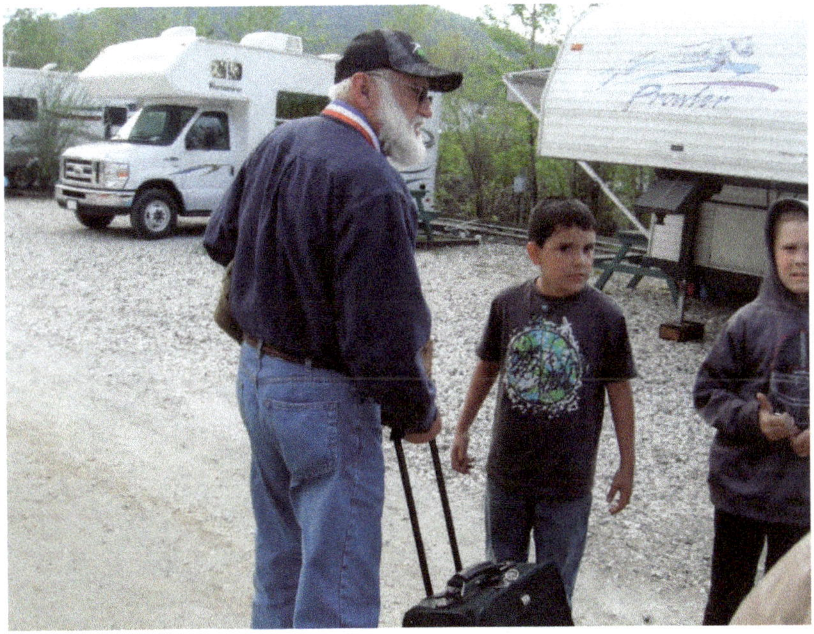
Prowler

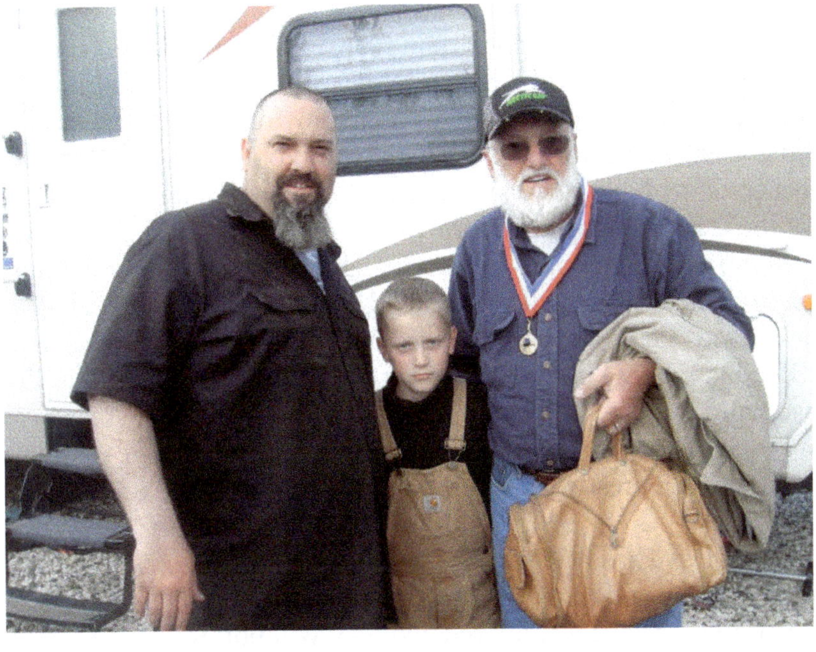

DAVE'S EXPLETIVE

    Without money for food, supplies and fuel, Todd's group was hard pressed ever since they left Sandy, Oregon. With the possible exception of DaveTurin (who is well off), they were not being paid in a timely fashion. Only once did Dave borrow funds from Kato – he needed Canadian currency. Although he forgot to monetarily repay Kato back, he was very generous with his personal time. Up to this point, no one ever had a bad word for Dave (he is a senior pastor where Todd attends services). Every morning in the Yukon, Dave got up early to prepare a hearty breakfast and spiritual food in reading and teaching the Scriptures. Occasionally, Jack and Kato go out for breakfast at a restaurant a couple of blocks away. I also stayed in Jack's RV. Blue didn't mind sharing his space with me. I bribed Blue by bringing a 5-gallon gravity food feeder and a sack of dry dog food. Oh yes, the bad word.

    While I sanded down metal plates with sharp and rough edges as James wanted me to do, he told me, "Get ready for an explosion." I replied, "What do you mean, James?"

    "Well, Kato, Dave has been supervising us to work on this important segment of getting the wash plant up and running. You see this conveyor belt system, Kato, the parts we have been waiting for have just arrived and they will not fit. Dave forgot to measure it (accurately) and weeks of work have gone down the drain. So Kato, stand back and get ready for the explosion."

I immediately dropped what I was working, located and told Tim Dalby ("the" cameraman) about the incoming artillery shell that was ready to explode. As Dave brought the long awaited parts from the delivery truck for the wash plant, Tim's camera crew was ready to capture his reaction. At the moment he realized the parts didn't fit, he belched out the loudest 4-letter word ever heard - everyone within 3 miles heard it. After Dave realized the camera and sound technicians captured what just transpired, his face turned from red to green and then blue. Dave later apologized to the cast members, RAW, Discovery and, to my understanding, the television audience.

WOOD BLOCK

A crucial situation arose involving a risky maneuver: the wash plant needed to be loaded by crane onto the 24-wheel transport at Wayne Fisher's property. The driver/loader called for a piece of wood to cushion/balance the heavy wash plant; everyone scrambled to look for one. When I found a block of wood, I ran over to give it to the loader/crane operator. Someone said later I ruined the shot that RAW was filming. Who knows and who cares.

I said, "Are they trying to get the job done at this critical maneuver, or are they trying to score points for dramatics?"

ANOTHER GOLD MINE?

Speaking of Wayne Fisher, he showed me large nuggets of gold that he found in his mine somewhere north of Dawson City. It was accessible by speedboat only, not riverboat or land. I took him up on the offer to look (acquire/film) at the location. The next day, Wayne rented a huey to take me, Todd and Jack for a tour of his mine. Of course RAW wanted to tag along again since it provided a good opportunity for filming. Sadly, there wasn't enough room in the helicopter for an additional cameraman, sound technician, and director – this was another missed opportunity for Discovery.

CLAIMS & MINE EQUIPMENT

- 52 CLAIMS INCLUDES WATER & LAND USE LICENSE
- 25 FT BY 8 ½ FT HERRING SKIFF
- TEST PLANT WITH VIBRATING SCREEN PLANT
- WASH PLANT WITH VIBRATING FEEDER & SCREEN DECK & SLUICE BOX
- 6" TRASH PUMP WITH CUMMINS 6 CYC ENGINE ON FRAME & SUCTION HOSE
- 6" HIGH PRESSURE PUMP, SUCTION & FOOT VALVE
- D9G CAT WITH S BLADE & DOUBLE RIPPER
- 48 FT DRY VAN TRAILER
- 36 FT SINGLE AXLE HI BOY TRAILER
- 1984 CHEV ½ TON 2 WHEEL DRIVE PICKUP
- 1990 GMC SUBURBAN 4X4
- 1973 INT HI WAY TRACTOR TANDOM /W 5TH WHEEL
- 235 CAT EXCAVATOR
- 1988 WA 450 KOMATSU LOADER
- 2008 20 FT RIPPLE RUNNER JET BOAT
- BIG 500 DIESEL WELDER & CABLES
- COMPRESSOR
- KUBOTA GEN SET 8 KLW
- D8K CAT WITH BLADE & RIPPER
- 3306 CAT ENGINE WITH 10" PUMP ON FRAME
- 14'X16' WOOD FRAME 2 MAN BUNKHOUSE
- 14'X16' WOOD FRAME COOKHOUSE
- 14'X14' NEW WOOD FRAME CABIN
- 24 FT TRAVEL TRAILER
- 1 - 3000 GAL FUEL TANK   2 - 1000 GAL FUEL TANKS
- 1 - 500 GAL FUEL TANK   1 - 10,000 GAL FUEL TANK
- 1 - 300 GAL FUEL TANK

LARGE SELECTION OF HAND & SHOP TOOLS & TORCHES
ALL KITCHEN EQUIPMENT & APPLIANCES

YUKON WATER BOARD

Pursuant to the *Waters Act* and *Waters Regulation*, the Yukon Water Board hereby grants a Type B water use licence for placer mining undertaking to:

Wayne Fischer
Box 632
Dawson City, YT Y0B 1G0

LICENCE NUMBER:	PM05-493		
LICENCE TYPE:	B	UNDERTAKING:	PLACER
WATER USE AREA:	02	STREAM CLASSIFICATION:	II/IV
LOCATION: Latitude:	62° 56' N	Longitude:	139° 09' W

WATER SOURCE: Sparkling Creek, a tributary of the Yukon River

MAXIMUM QUANTITY: 8,730 cubic metres per day

EFFECTIVE DATE: The effective date of this licence shall be the date on which the signature of the Chairperson of the Yukon Water Board is affixed.

EXPIRY DATE: January 1, 2016

This licence shall be subject to the restrictions and conditions contained herein, and to the restrictions and conditions contained in the *Waters Act* and the *Waters Regulation* made thereunder.

Dated this 13 day of June, 2006

Witness

Approved by:

Chairperson
YUKON WATER BOARD

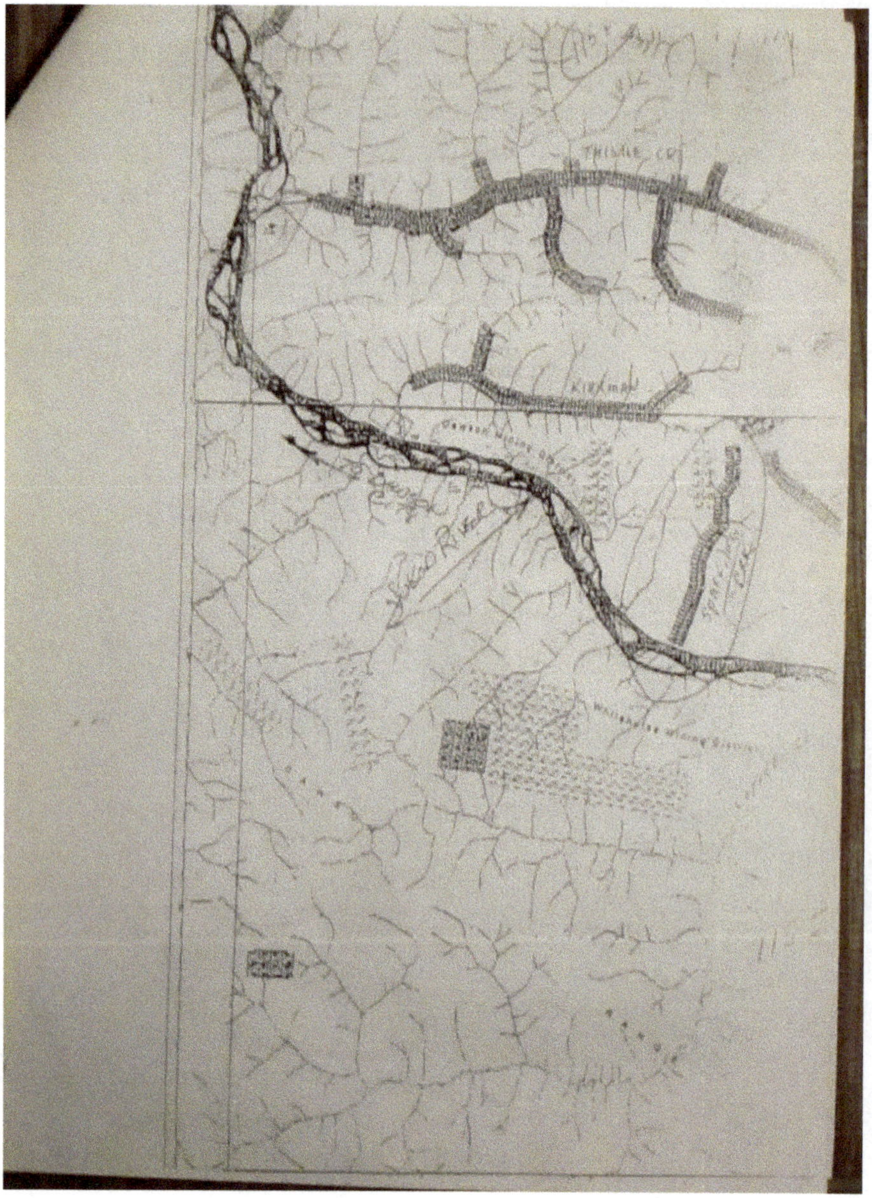
THISTLE CR
KIRKMAN

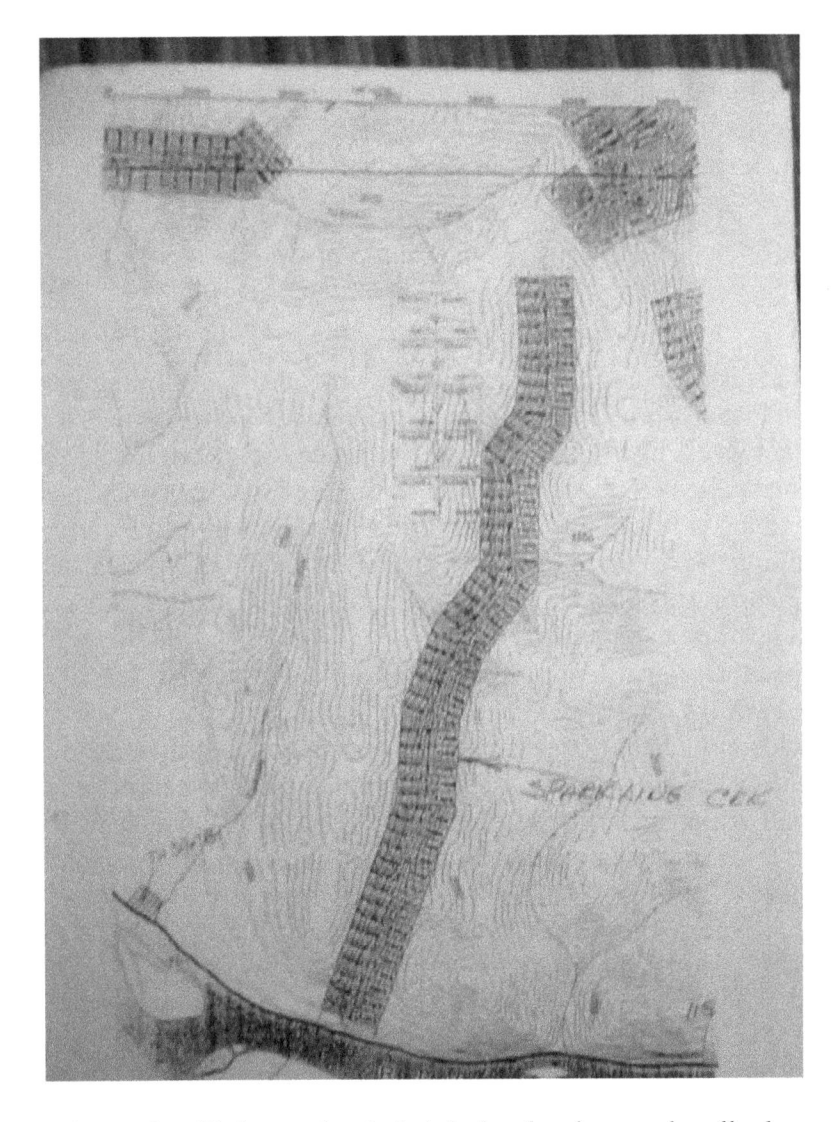

After an hour plus flight, we landed right by the river and walked up a trail. It was truly a magnificent locale: the mountains in the background, a roaring river, wind and snow-washed buildings, fuel tanks and heavy equipment poised to spit out gold ore at the signal of a .45 caliber gun blast. To me, this was what real modern-day gold mining should look like. We were expecting Humphrey Bogart's Fred C. Dobbs of "The Treasure of the Sierra Madre" to come out behind the rocky crevasse and greet us. The only question we needed to know was whether there was enough gold there to make it worth our while. I'm afraid this is a story for another time. When we returned, I asked the pilot to make a couple of low-level strafes at RAW and our men.

Todd might have been overcharged by Wayne for equipment, supplies, fuel, and certainly, the roadside wash plant. During the 1849 California Gold Rush, most prospectors never found any gold and instead lost money (and their lives). The real 49er gold miners were the likes of Leland Stanford, Andrew Carnegie and Levi Strauss - suppliers. In jest, Todd said that "Wayne mines the miners."

SOPORIFIC

After what turned out to be a long and uneventful day of filming guys repairing the wash plant at Fisher's property, some of us prepared to go to Gertie's for a nice dinner. Earlier that week, I gave Dave a long and needed rubdown to loosen his tired muscles. In doing so, he verbalized a thirty-plus minute rendition of his massage experience he and his wife had in Thailand (if my memory serves me correctly as to the country). In addition to providing logistical, financial, legal and physical security, I also wore the hat of a last resort medic. I brought medical supplies and equipment to address anything from a tick bite to a bear bite.

Since I had the reputation of being serious all the time (and since it was getting a bit boring), Todd always wanted me to loosen up by telling a joke or two. So to liven things up, I quickly applied a double carotid maneuver on Dave. I waited for him to motion me to release the hold. In his usual trueheartedness, Dave didn't even let out a whimper of sound or flap his arms. After a few more moments, which probably seemed like an eternity for Dave, I released the hold. He just smiled while everyone else couldn't believe what just took place.

"I apologize now, Dave, if I caught you off guard. I don't know if that compression I administered cause you to be soporific or not."

As usual, you're always terrific and a good sport, further testament of your sense of humor.

LOST SUPPLIES

After a short while, Jack left Dawson City to recover the kitchen/cooking/equipment trailer that was stopped at the Canadian border. According to some, the wet/snowing spring roads have yet to thaw; this caused traction issues. I was told that all the supplies therein were given to the indigent. I have personally witnessed Todd's charitable traits in Oregon and throughout the trip. I'm not sure if there was a motivation of Canadian taxation on the "importation" of food, supplies and equipment beyond immediate, normal and personal use. I knew thousands of dollars of much needed supplies were lost, painstakingly selected and purchased for the sole benefit of satisfying the duality of the trip, - i.e., (1) accomplishment of the mission and (2) welfare of the men.

A tax would have been levied against items to be brought into Canada if it were to be resold for profit, a contention that must be proven by the carrier (you're guilty, prove your innocence). Nevertheless, it was our loss and someone's (needful) gain.

This is partial list of caloric items what EACH was mandated to bring overland 120 years ago before one was allowed to proceed into the Klondike:

Flour	800 lbs.
Corn Meal	200
Bacon	200
Beans	150
Dried Fruits	150
Sugar	75
Coffee	75
Rice	50
Condensed Milk	1 case

Central business district of a mining town

BIGGER HEADS

With the success of Gold Rush taking top ratings not only on the Discovery Channel (but also the biggest hit in Friday television), each cast members' public image grew. Many autograph and photo hounds found their mark wherever Gold Rush cast members appeared - local stores, restaurants, gas stations, etc., and eventually at paid appearances in conventions and corporate events ($25,000 price tag for speaking engagements). Many carried a stash of unsigned Discovery photo handouts in their portfolios/vehicles to autograph and satiate a ravenous crowd. Every cast member knew personal time in front of the camera translated into renegotiated, higher-paying contracts. Personal appearances and public and commercial endorsements fatten their wallets.

As stated previously, Todd later took a "little less" money from Discovery in exchange for heavy equipment. Other demands were in lieu of "external" (later internal) funding and outside investors. Striking or work stoppages by Todd during the second season proved to be an effective tactic then and perhaps in other seasons (expensive relocation to South America is a clear example of external funding, i.e. Discovery Channel).

STURGEON

Remember the Jimmy Stewart movie "The Flight of the Phoenix?" I was in the "Plight of the Sturgeon." Nicknamed for the label on the 9-seat GMC SUV, it was used and filmed extensively in season one. When I received notification that a very dear friend was dying, I asked Todd to borrow the Sturgeon to go home and return it back fully loaded with equipment and relief supplies.

sturge n
GIMME A GO FISHING ADVENTURES
CHEVROLET
OQL 776

sturgeon salmon

That wagon could literally hold tons of equipment and supplies. Regretfully, I didn't make it in time as my friend passed on to glory. After the funeral, I returned to Sandy and quickly loaded it up with everything that was designated and warehoused at the airport, this included Jack's Honda electric generator. Once fully loaded, I made my way back up to the Yukon by myself. While still in Oregon, I began to feel a little "play" in the steering wheel but thought nothing of it until it worsen near the U.S.-Canadian border. While stopped, the custom agents wanted to exam everything in the Sturgeon. After an hour went by, they woke me from my nap and allowed me to resume my trek. I had to restore my disheveled boxes in the Sturgeon before resuming my 65-hour trek from the lower 48 states. Fearing theft of property I was responsible for, I didn't stay in any hotels. In addition, I had to keep a tight schedule in reaching gas stations as they only opened during limited daylight hours. Insofar as the play in the steering was gradually getting worse, it became a real challenge staying on the right side of the road. On a lonely stretch of a deserted mountain road, the Sturgeon finally became too much to handle. A slight turn one way pulled me across to the extreme side of the road. Although I was crawling at 15 mph it didn't keep the Sturgeon straight. After two incursions into the right shoulder of the road, the third was the charmer - the Sturgeon went into the right shoulder knee deep in weeds and brush.

    Cell phone coverage was totally wishful thinking. I crawled out onto the road. After what seemed to be an eternity, a short caravan of three vehicles saw me flagging them on the road. They stopped and rendered assistance. These locals were very helpful and knew what to do. In a short time, a tow truck pulled the fully loaded Sturgeon back on the road and then onto its back. It carried me to a small village. After staying until the next morning, I hitchhiked a couple of hundred miles. I got off and looked to purchase another truck in another small community. All that was available was a dingy red, rusted pickup with a stick clutch. I never had to drive one but I quickly learned. After a half-dozen restarts, the $1,000 truck got me going.

Believe it or not, when I drove to a gas station many miles down the road, I recognized a Cadillac SUV - it looked like the same model that Wayne Fisher owned, even down to the crack on the windshield (unsurprisingly, it's rare to find an unbroken front windshield considering that gravel roads permeate the Yukon). Something extraordinary happens. Wayne Fisher comes out of the front entrance of the service station and does a double take as he couldn't believe seeing me there too. Bear in mind that this was not the regular road one would take, but the seldom-driven scenic route. Wayne and I were driving in the opposite direction on a very secluded back road of upper British Columbia.

As usual, Wayne comes to the rescue. He drops what he was doing and helped me. I got back to Dawson City in one piece, always in good spirit. The next thing was to drop these supplies off to Todd and then go back and make a second run to pick-up the other half of the remaining supplies. Another fully loaded circular trip was successfully completed a couple of days later.

FINGER POINTING

Since I needed to retrieve the abandoned red truck in White Horse, (approximately 300-400 miles from Dawson City), I also decided to report the status of the procurement of our own television channel to Todd, which we discussed at great lengths during my stay at the Yukon. I said that there was ample room for optimism. To help seek significant outside financial backing, I told Todd that I needed something unique to "open doors", much like my turn-of-the-century Gold Rush walking stick gift to Jack earlier. I suggested and Todd agreed that gold mined from the Yukon by his crew members would be considered unique.

I asked that the gold that was to be given be accompanied by photographs. I waited while Todd returned with the gold and my camera. I suggested two to three vials and Todd gives four. I asked the guys earlier if I could take a photo of them since I had never taken one with all of them together collectively. Instead, they dragged and placed me next to them and shot away (Kato is camera shy). I did not realize the content of the shots made until I had them developed when I got back home.

Unscripted

Re-shooting scripted

Third shoot. Got it finally - scripted photography.

The camera I brought was my only one, a $50 Nikon I found years ago in my (San Diego) hotel room safe. It was left by a previous occupant (the hotel wouldn't hold it for their lost and found since no claim was ever made). By the quality of photos taken, you can see that I'm no professional.

    After resuming my discussions with Todd, everyone bid fare well and returned to work. I asked Todd where Greg was and he told me that he "sent him home because of his alcoholism", not what Discovery said was his return to Oregon to look for work.

    Instead of immediately returning back down to the lower 48 states as planned, I met a professional guide who set me up with a turn-key hunt, much like what Jim Thurber did as a professional guide in the past (including one client by the name of John Wayne!). While looking for moose, the guide took me to an area that, by sheer coincidence, was just a few miles past Todd's mining site. After blowing and changing a flat tire, we came to this creek/wooded area and less than an hour later, we spotted moose. He handed me a high-power rifle as we stalked it. I took aim and began to squeeze the trigger when I had picture sight. I then immediately lowered the barrel. The guide asked me why. I said, "I couldn't shoot the moose because it was female."

    We returned the same route past the Gold Rush mining site and stopped for some target practice just within spitting distance. I left my calling card on the tree - newly fired bullet holes. In Dawson City, I told the guys it was Kato firing away. I hope I didn't interrupt RAW's filming with gun shots blasting in the background.

No, I didn't do it - road kill on my trip up.

Another unfortunate road kill from the trip back into British Columbia

MONEY OVER MATTER

Previously, I had mentioned that Todd was difficult to reach. I returned to the mining site for further deliberation. Discovery happened to have some of its management on location and did not welcome my presence outside. While in consultation with Todd outside the actual mining site, Discovery implored RAW repeatedly to get him back to the shoot. Todd waved his hand to stop bothering us. After forty-five minutes of consultation, I left Todd in an optimistic manner along with a few of my personal items that I left behind (medical textbooks and some DVDs). It was at this time that suggestion/request of furnishing actual gold mined here was acquiesced by Todd for the purpose of "giving good gifts" as door openers to certain investors; this was needed to back the organization of our new television channel.

I cannot know whether Discovery caught wind of our intentions to supplant them with another cable channel; it had been discussed that they wanted to put a lid on that idea by removing Todd from any affiliation with BATTLEGROUND so that he would not be further distracted with that endeavor. In return, they compensated him financially for that consideration. At the expense of the BATTLEGROUND partnership, this tactic would have certainly yielded more leverage with Todd in the form of compensation and perhaps, content and/or control.

For the sake of money, Todd turned his back on those relationships he professed to hold. For example, the joint and equal partnership BATTLEGROUND reality television show that he co-founded with Mike Fox, U.S. Olympian Dan Russell, which was later funded by Kato, was dropped by Todd when he was pressured and compensated by Discovery (a competing show by another network may induce a conflict of interest to this channel). He gave up his 25% interest to Dan. Todd later acquiesced to represent BATTLEGROUND, for whom a major pilot was produced with luminaries that included "The Expendables'(1,2, and 3)" Randy Couture, who, for a major fee, would serve as an executive producer.

After Todd left the partnership (paid by Discovery to leave Bonhoeffer LLC, according to Mike Fox) that Dan became 50% owner. After my visit and discussions with Todd at the Yukon mining site and in Dawson City (along with other considerable meetings), Mike Fox told me Todd gave up his partnership of BATTLEGROUND by selling out to Discovery. It took too much time and detracted attention away from Gold Rush when Todd was soliciting not only Discovery, but other TV channels on behalf of BATTLEGROUND. In exchange for forfeiting partnership and representing BATTLE-GROUND, I was told that Todd was remunerated, financially as well as with heavy mining equipment. So much for outside investors.

Later, Dan and/or Mike said Todd would use his influence in helping BATTLEGROUND to get on TV by becoming an executive producer/consultant. Remuneration for such services was rumored to be approximately tens of thousands of dollars. In any event, Todd benefited and the partnership lost. With a deep sigh some time later it was told that "Todd would take BATTLEGROUND to other channels as a talent producer for about $25,000."

INNER SANCTUM

I spent many weeks/months and evenings in Todd's RV. It was the largest and best equipped RV up there - did he get that for free too? We talked endlessly about everything for hours – from financial to personal. Oh yes, we watched "Napoleon Dynamite" if the other guys could tolerate it. As far as I could tell, only James and Greg's RV had a DVD player, maybe Dave's too. Greg's son was in the RV and Mrs. Turin was also in theirs. So Todd's RV, with his kids sometime, became the logical focus of meetings and fellowship. Anyway, Todd was the one who called the shots. When Todd and I were the only ones inside the RV, he shared some very private secrets.

PRODUCT PLACEMENT

Products placed on the show have had significantly higher retail sales as a result of free publicity and endorsed use by the cast members. In turn, Todd received significant amounts of merchandise. Some were given to guys accordingly. The products given to Todd and placed in the show included everything imaginable; outdoor clothing, cold weather gear, Arctic Cat ATVs, hats, weapons, mosquito repellents, and so forth. Among others as I have confirmed to date: James received a .50 caliber Magnum Research semi-automatic, which he later traded for another pistol and cash.

HIT & RUN

Everything was on schedule as RAW filmed Gold Rush. By renting a helicopter, they made great aerial shots; the RAW crew was livid in just about everything they captured. During this time, the driver/cameraman and a director "escorted" me around while in actuality, kept me away from interrupting the shoot (Remember James Carter's role of keeping Lee busy in "Rush Hour"). As this team was about to capture a special scene, the cameraman stood up through the sunroof to get a better shot - I was told to hold onto him by grabbing and clutching onto his belt. This was the same team that later drove their vehicle on Wayne Fisher's property and wanted to play "chicken" with me as I stood there snapping still shots of my own.

I was "accidentally" hit by them when I was standing still. I don't know if he hit me accidentally or if it was a deliberate attempt to stop or intimidate me from taking behind the scenes photos. I wasn't hiding but out in the open (as usual) taking snap shots. Whether they were playing around, "sending a message" tacitly or just following orders, I was bumped on the left side of my left leg as he was inching forward towards me. It wasn't a straight, nonstop movement but a stop-and-go motion with his vehicle - i.e., stopping closer by the foot and then by inches. Unfortunately, the last stop hit me. I'm not sure that they realize that my cargo pants' pockets contained items (wallet, passport, etc.) causing a protrusion/bulge, thus hitting it and then me. All of a sudden I experienced excruciating pain that seemed to explode throughout my lower extremity and then beyond. Without realizing what actually took place, the vehicle retreated and the occupants were laughing and smiling. I went to the Fisher house dragging my left leg and sat down on their porch grimacing in pain.

When Todd heard about my "accident", he got fuming mad. In our previous discussions in his RV (which took place after a typical day's shoot), he mentioned that RAW's god was their career, their work, their profession - the singularly most important thing in their lives. If they got fired, their whole life would be destroyed. They would lose not only their entire investment of time and fortune (as you might say) but also a livelihood for themselves and support for their family back in England. Therefore, if Todd complained to Discovery about RAW's role in my injury, then that would surely cause someone's head to roll.

Todd understood my predicament and, foaming at the mouth, was ready to go to bat for me by getting that guy's head served on a platter. I suggested to him not to cause someone to lose their job and perhaps his life-long career permanently. That individual's eternal salvation is more important than my leg injury. Some of the other guys, like James, disagreed. Upon learning of my "accident" James just stood there, not smiling. I can see a little white water vapor coming out of his ears. He thought that the driver and passenger/supervisor should be reprimanded and sent home for playing with the dangerous weapon of a vehicle. Others intimated that it was a deliberate action to remove me from the film set. From the beginning, Discovery wanted me to sign waivers, releases and other documents. I complied but they kept coming back for more.

raw TV

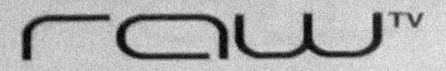

Name:

Address:

Date:

Dear **Name:**

Gold Rush, The Series ("the Production")

This letter is to confirm the terms on which we are prepared to disclose/discuss the details of the Production to/with you.

For the purposes of this letter 'Confidential Information' means all information of whatever nature in whatever form relating to the Production obtained from any source including without limitation information received from the Company and information obtained as a result of being allowed access to any premises where the Company may carry on business but does not extend to information which at the time it is obtained is in the public domain.

For good and valuable consideration, you warrant undertake and agree as follows:

1. You shall treat all Confidential Information as being strictly private and confidential and shall take all steps necessary to prevent it from being disclosed or made public to any third party or coming by any means into the possession of any third party.

2. You shall use the Confidential Information solely for the purpose of evaluating whether or not to enter into an agreement with the Company relating to the Production or to perform any obligations which you may undertake or have undertaken with the Company relating to the Production and you shall not use any part of the Confidential Information for any other purpose whatsoever.

3. You shall not use or disclose or permit the disclosure by any person of the Confidential Information for the benefit of any third party or in such a way as to procure a commercial advantage over the Company.

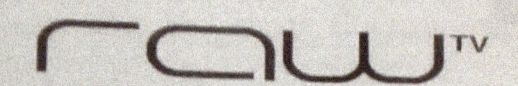

> **raw** TV
>
> 4. The Confidential Information and its circulation shall be restricted to circulation and disclosure to individuals whose identity shall have been approved by the Company prior to disclosure in writing.
>
> 5. You shall keep all materials containing Confidential Information in a safe and secure place and return them to the Company immediately on determination of our discussions in relation to the Production or on the Company's prior request.
>
> 6. You undertake to indemnify and keep the Company at all times fully indemnified from and against any loss or disclosure of Confidential Information and from all actions proceedings claims demands costs awards and damages however arising as a result of any breach or non-performance of any of the warranties undertakings or obligations under this agreement.
>
> Yours sincerely
>
>
> (signature on behalf of Company)
>
>
>
> (signature of owner)
> I agree and confirm the above and agree to be bound by it.

    Todd did not want Discovery to interfere with my invitation to accompany him and Jack. I responded throughout my stay by replying to Discovery in the same fashion as any hire in the Cabinet - "I serve at the pleasure of the President." "I serve at the pleasure of the Hoffmans." End of discussion.

    Through my insistence, it was decided not to bring it to RAW's higher authority nor mention it any further. Jack was vehement towards the driver and supervisor while Chris and Greg rolled their eyes in disbelief. Although Todd's team wanted the situation to be brought to RAW's management, the decision was ultimately mine.

    When I got back home I sought out physical therapy and everything under the sun (short of surgery). Surgery was always the last resort. Without much pain mediation for months, I resigned myself to the knife. With the skillful art and reliable hands of Oakland Raiders head team physician, Dr. Warren King, he performed his usual miracles to get his stars back into the game (of life). Seen on one of the walls in his Palo Alto medical office (among a plethora of awards and photos from his illustrious and appreciative patients) is an autographed Discovery Channel photo of the Gold Rush team and another Gold Rush team photo that I was in with my inscription of:

"Hit the ground running one day after surgery with no PT.
Thanks for the best YAC in the NFL!"

"YAC" for those few novices on Mars means the most important stat for receivers, Yards After Catch. Dave Turin played wide out receiver in high school varsity, just like luminary Jerry Rice - the greatest in that position and, arguably, one of the greatest ever to play in the NFL.

I think you might like to know how tough Dave really is, as everyone already knows on Gold Rush. A caveat: "Don't ever mess around with this dude or you'll regret it." I love to have Dave lead me through dark alleys, literally and figuratively.

96

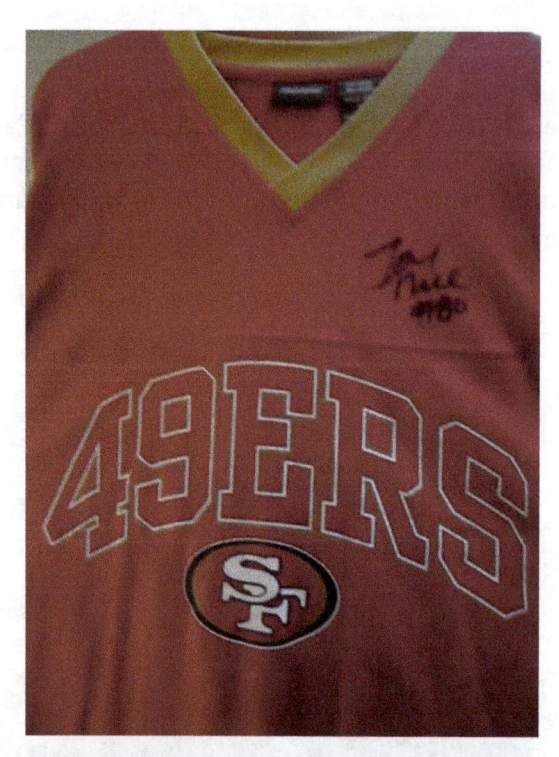

CONFESSION

When Todd and I returned to the Sandy Airport in June, he confessed to me how troubled he had become. Despite Gold Rush's success, the ramifications of being criticized and verbally attacked was overwhelming.

When I first told Todd that he needed to delegate some of the duties and responsibilities he had been inundated with, he quipped quickly and I kept reminding him and parole evidenced again. Todd attempted to respond to literally every member of his television audience. They emailed him and he responded likewise - such a Herculean task. He told me (and later publicly) that viewers asked him if they could join his noble venture to go to Alaska/Yukon. Some even wrote saying they were from as far away as the Northeast to the Florida coast.

How can he respond to such audience loyalty? On the other side of the coin, Todd also got emailed with criticism from both here and abroad. It even got to the point of downright ridicule. I'm not going to repeat those words of sarcasm. I don't know whether he even responded to them, but I'm sure they would have indelibly left their mark physically, mentally and spiritually. Todd's eyes welled up.

When I used to phone call a member of the "4 Musketeers" (Todd, Dan, Mike and Kato) to check on the progress of "BATTLEGROUND", Rev. Dan Russell, former U.S. Olympian wrestler who was destined to win the gold medal, told me about the discussion I had that day with Todd. He told Dan that his spirit was lifted and renewed from what I said. This is what I said to him.

"Whatever effort you put forth in Gold Rush, whatever mountains you have to move, whatever fiery darts of criticism comes at you, remember Luke 15: 7 & 10."

OLD GLORY

As everyone already knows (at least now the reading public herein), Todd had always been generous with not only his time but in giving good gifts. One of the most profound things that had ever happened to me was when Todd and I returned to the Sandy Airport. He presented a flag to me, one that was actually flown over the U.S. Capitol. He knew the significance I placed on Old Glory. Todd knows how to give gifts too. I have mementos that carry little intrinsic value but have huge historical significance; this includes a sheet of U.S. postage stamps commemorating the flag raising on Mount Suribachi on the Japanese island of Iwo Jima – it was autographed by Joseph Rosenthal, the Pulitzer Prize photographer who captured that momentous event.

Sidebar. Although Associated Press photographer Rosenthal (who later worked for the San Francisco Chronicle) for years was forced to deny erroneous reports that he personally STAGED the second flag raising and attempted to pass it off as the original first flag raising, it was actually captured by Marine Corp photographer Sgt. Louis R. Lowery of Sgt. Ernest I. Thomas, Jr. on the morning of 23 February 1945.

Pfc. Rene A. Gagnon, PM3/c John H. Bradley, Pfc. Ira H. Hayes
Iwo Jima flag raisers

CLINT EASTWOOD MOMENT

After the knee operation, I attended the wedding of Mike Fox's son, Talon, a most talented individual that you would want to work with, much like his father. Upon arrival at the Sandy church, I was asked by Todd's son to join him inside the main chapel. After the ceremony we were invited to the reception at the Sandy Airport auditorium/hunting lodge where Jack, gracious as usual, provided the ambiance of the facilities for the overflowing crowd.

The three of us sat there while the crowd just walked by and stared at them (Jack and Todd). "Another (Clint) Eastwood moment" I said to myself.

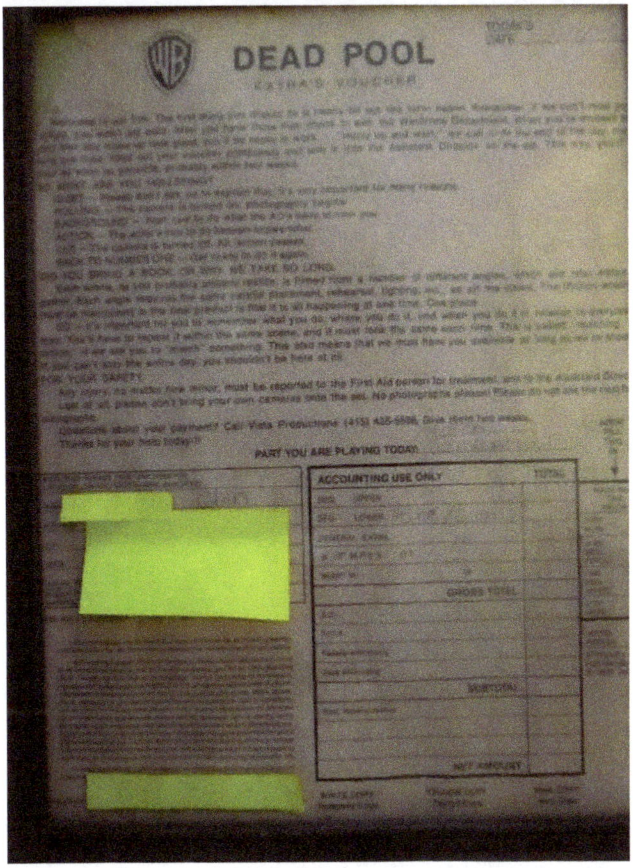

DEAD POOL

EXTRA'S VOUCHER

FOR YOUR SAFETY

Thanks for your help today!!

PART YOU ARE PLAYING TODAY:

ACCOUNTING USE ONLY	TOTAL
GROSS TOTAL	
SUBTOTAL	
NET AMOUNT	

I use this metaphor because of a charity function held at and benefiting Gavilan College near Monterey (Gilroy to be exact), when the star luminary appeared with mounted sheriff deputies escorting him in. With notable personalities from the sporting and political world, everybody's head in the auditorium turned towards Clint as he walked in - they stood steadfast. Realizing what was happening, I observed that nobody wanted to disturb him, leaving him standing alone for the longest minute as he was trying to hold his smile. Finally, I walked over and broke the ice by shaking hands with him and exchanging the usual platitudes. After a few minutes and getting a bit role in his last "Dirty Harry" movie series, people started to swarm all over him for photos and autographs.

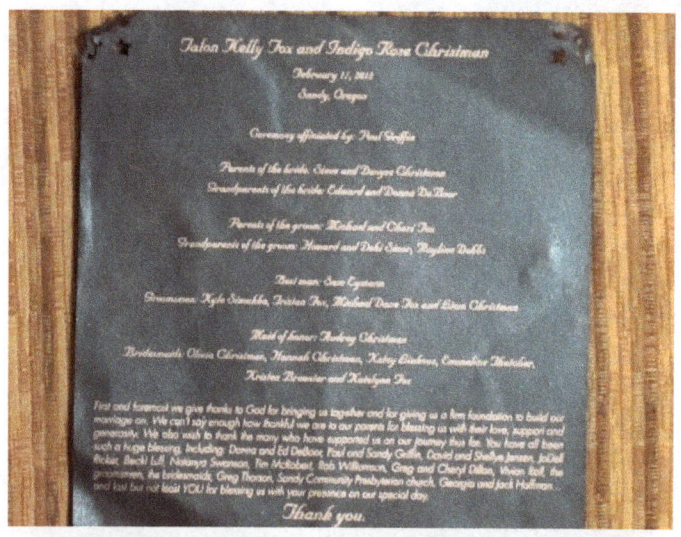

After we were joined by the groom and bride, they finally broke the hosts' "Eastwood" star power of Todd and Jack.

100

Todd and I sneaked out for Outback Steakhouse, where we were joined by the Thurbers. After the usual great steaks and fellowship, Todd pulled out a knife and began to give verbal instructions on the operation of the blade. Not realizing what it was leading to, he handed it over and said it now belonged to me. Unbeknownst to me, my mouth had dropped open - I was speechless in response to his customary generosity. The waitress was tipped a $1, $5, $10 and a $20 bill to make sure that she remembered that Gold Rush was here.

RE-SHOOTING SCRIPT

While Todd and Kato were eating at an Alaskan restaurant, Todd received on his phone/computer the contractual agreement of $250,000 in exchange for personal endorsements, promotions and appearances on behalf of a Texas gold company owner. I believe this agreement was arranged by Mike Fox. After reading it, I told Todd that it placed him at liability if the company was sued from enraged investors or defaulted buyers if gold plunges from the high that it was at - $1,700 at that time to a tad above $1,000, an over 40% drop.

Throughout all the contractual obligations he would have needed to fulfill, Todd would be the public face representing a private company that faced possible individual, group or class-action lawsuits and thus be named along with the rest of the defendants. Surely it would mean the end of the Gold Rush show for the Hoffmans as well as possible personal bankruptcy. Todd readily took my recommendation under advisement and declined to accept it. He then had to backtrack episodes to reshape the Gold Rush plot. Since RAW had already shot and Discovery had already aired those episodes, a re-shoot was needed.

By accepting my recommendations that the Texas investor be not tapped as a source of funds, they filmed Todd "making phone calls" - (holding a phone to his ear? From the Sandy Airport office annex across from Todd's house.) I watched as the camera crew kept filming over and over again until they got it right. So much for reality (TV).

STANFORD

While I stayed in Jack Hoffman's RV, I and others heard loud snoring emanating from the other RV that was shared by Chris and Jim Thurber. Jim stayed out late at night, not for entertainment or dinner at Gertie's, but out of necessity. The snoring kept him up at night; he was losing sleep. On occasion, I saw Chris grab the side of his face and ear with his hand. I asked him why and he just smiled in response. I repeated my question when I saw him grabbing the side of his face again. He relented by saying that he had a tumor inside. I was dumbfounded.

The next day, I consulted with Wayne Fisher about the acquisition of an RV in the Dawson area. None were available except possibly in nearby Whitehorse, 300-plus miles away. Soon thereafter, Wayne informed me of two that had become available. He later acquired them. I asked Chris to accompany me and pick one for himself. Chris thanked me and offered to construct a cabin once I acquire the lumber. The RV provided Chris with privacy, pride of ownership, and quietness for Jim to dream at night - and, as they might say, "Killed two birds with one stone."

When Chris and his wife dropped over to my neck of the woods in San Francisco, I lodged them at Union Square's St. Francis, the residence of kings, queens and presidents for over a century. After a nice weekend of playing tourist and eating at Harris' Restaurant, Fisherman's Grotto #9, North Beach's Mona Lisa #3, plus Chinatown and

Little Saigon, we went to Stanford and also dropped by to greet my orthopedic surgeon, Dr. Warren King. After the examination in Stanford it was determined that Chris' tumor was benign – his hearing restored with some minor aide.

Between seasonal shoots, Chris was asked by Discovery's head man of off-season treatment of his hearing impairment. Chris said that "it was one of the show's fans who referred him to Stanford University Medical Center." He pressed Chris for a name-____ .

SACRIFICIAL LAMB

Todd's 100 oz. goal failed not because of inefficiencies caused by a lackadaisical or AWOL mechanic - James Harness was chosen as the sacrificial lamb. James was indignant for being portrayed as unprofessional (by Discovery) on this international show.

For example, James told me that once, he was in a hurry and needed his vehicle serviced. He returned hours later and discovered that they didn't even change the filters. Since James is certified in the automobile industry as a real professional, he pointed out their deficiencies. The service representative refused to acknowledge their mistakes and got too close into James' face. James politely knocked him out and was subsequently released without charges or incident by police. Remember, James said to me,

"As a professional, I gave Todd a set of suggestions or recommendations (to) be reviewed for more proper undertaking of our mining operation. It would be (deemed) appropriate for the public to see me and the rest of Todd's group no longer as greenhorns but as real miners."

When Todd failed to follow in any significant recommendations offered by James, it was decided by James to leave Gold Rush and all the glory that went with the show. The notoriety the show brought was not enough to overcome his own pride. James had to look himself in the mirror every morning and knew that the temporary wealth and glory it brought would pale to insignificance in the short run.

Knowing that James was going to leave, Discovery and/or Todd wanted some extra mileage and decided to use James whatever way they could on the show, even if by the use of false intimation (as was the case). Suggestion was made for the "firing" of James after it was learned that there was a possible gold shortage (after its weighing in the tent room). Todd's whole season was centered around getting the 100 ounce goal, which was about ten times more than their first season in Alaska. At the end of each episode, Discovery previewed the next show with a cliffhanger or sneak preview to whet the hungry appetite of the audience. That preview revealed what appeared to be the last person seen in the tent area - it "showed" James. The very next episode revealed nothing whatsoever of James or anyone else absconding gold!

To this very date, a lot of the loyal Gold Rush audience are upset with this false portrayal of James and are boycotting this show by watching either Tom Selleck in "Blue Bloods" or "Hawaii Five-0" Friday evenings in the same time slot.

James found this singular footage most despicable and couldn't cope with it until a year and a half had gone by. To help forget the bad taste in his mouth and find some modicum of peace, James sold the .50 caliber Magnum Research pistol given to him by Todd and gave his entire first season's worth of gold to Kato.

By telling the Discovery audience that they were short of their 100 ounce goal by only a few ounces, and then finding a scapegoat by pointing a finger of blame to one individual is hypocrisy.

As James used to say, "When you point your finger at someone, three fingers are always pointing back at yourself."

To further demonstrate the failure of reaching the 100 ounce goal as their mainstay byline every week, Todd gave Kato four tubes of gold for the purpose of using them as door openers for soliciting financing for Todd and Kato's new television channel. When you add this amount of gold given to Kato to the total you would have reached the 100 ounce goal. But instead, Discovery/Todd manipulated Gold Rush viewers to return for another season.

CHRIS & GREG TALK

Two men who are living the American dream...are full of hope, a belief in their own abilities and a deep faith in God as they work to control their destinies. Last week's episode marked the beginning of their third season in the hunt for their own bonanza in the Yukon. Their story is similar to so many other stories in the present economy. Chris and Greg live in an area that's depressed like so many others. So what did six men do? They sold everything they could, bought some used equipment and headed north looking for the opportunity to work and maybe find gold.

"We started mining even before TV ever got on board so we're not mining for television," said Greg.

"We're mining for the future and basically the way the economy is going, still, I haven't seen any evidence to change my mind. What's that mean for gold?" he asked as he pointed a thumb upward.

"That's why we're mining. The jobs that were available ten years ago in construction aren't available anymore. The jobs that were available five years ago, they're gone. There's too many people standing in line waiting for help, and we're getting on our own horse and going for it ourselves. That's basically what's the premise for the show is structured on and that's what we believe that's the way we're wired."

"The one piece of the gold that none of us really experienced was the actual capturing of the gold," Greg said. "It's placer mining; we use a wash plant, generally various other pieces of equipment, panning is involved. When we see what's pay dirt, you pan it, test it, once there's enough color in it you get to the sluice box."

"We try to get up there in the spring, once it thaws out," he says.

"Two things shut us down in the fall: we run out of pay dirt and we don't have enough ground exposed or the weather - things start freezing up. And when it freezes up to the point where the wash plant doesn't work anymore or the ground freezes in big chunks and it doesn't break down, it's time to go home."

"The first season, we got just under 15 ounces. We learned a lot but it didn't do much for us. The second season, we just got under 94 ounces so we're getting better."

Chris said, "Our knowledge and understanding of mining has grown to the point of where being a successful gold miner is now very attainable."

"As the years have gone on and our mining experience, our equipment grew and we started getting investors."

"People are starting to take risks on us now. They think we can turn a profit. We have proven ourselves to be effective, and it depends on what the ground holds. People are willing to invest in us."

"It's the way the economy is, it's the way the country is going," Chris declared.

"It's not the location, it's a state of mind, it's an opportunity, find a passion, chase it, make a living out of it. Personally, I'm hoping Romney makes it because he's for small business; I've seen a lot of small business get brutalized in the past few years by government."

"We have a generation that doesn't understand. And we have an administration that creates jobs that cost the working man. Romney supports business. I'm glad he supports the rich because the rich provide jobs for the working man and woman. Turn the government jobs over to the private sector."

"One of the things we're allowing TV to film what we do is to encourage the American man to get out, find his passion, pursue it, don't be afraid of failure."

"We failed the first year miserably. So pick yourself up, you brush yourself off and you hit it again. That's what made this country strong and I think we need to do that again. We can't sit back and wait for the government to take care of us."

In Canada, "they say this is a violation, you need to fix it, here's the best way to fix, how much time do you think you'll need to fix it. Three days? We'll be back in five or email us a picture of the repair. They work with you."

Greg said, "We want to share our faith in God to give people hope for the future whether it's spiritual or something tangible."

"Get off our butts, make something happen for yourself. We're doing it, we're trying. We get notes, letters, emails from all over the world saying things like I've been motivated to save my company, watching a program which we know that's from a higher power than ourselves."

"We're just fumbling idiots trying to do something to support ourselves and our families and we're ordinary men trying to do something extraordinary and that's what it's all about. Whether or not we hit the mother lode, whether or not we become rich, those things are sidelines to why we're really doing this."

Chris said, "I was asked what have I gotten out of it. I wished I'd have taken more chances. I was always afraid of starting my own business because of what friends and family might think of me...not the risk but of what others might think of me. I'd wish I'd had the courage to cast that aside and say this is my passion. I can make it work if I work hard enough. I don't want handouts. I'm going to do this on my own."

"That's what I've gotten out of the last three years. To see these guys with nothing. I walked in to six broken down men and a broken down wash plant, but they had a goal; they had a desire; they had a passion and I got caught up in it. I've got to jump in and do what I can to help out and you just put your heart into something like that, it's hard for it to fail."

At the conclusion, we were asked to participate in a Romney For President election rally. We respectfully declined to be opening act presenters instead of appearing onstage with the presidential candidate as endorsers.

CHRIS QUITS

According to Wikipedia, provided by a legal representative, it shows the following:

Chris Doumitt, age 59, originally he was only meant to come to Alaska for ten days - to help build a cabin for Greg Remsburg and his family. But gold mining quickly got under his skin and he ended up staying for five months and becoming a key member of the team. He calls himself a 'pumpologist.' Chris retired from the Hoffman crew after season 3. In season 4 and season 5, he worked for Parker Schnabel."

Chris tells me two reasons for leaving Gold Rush at the conclusion of the third season.

When the host asked why he was leaving, Chris said (without his usual smile, as the camera panned in on Todd) that it was time to move on with his life. Attention then went to Greg and he responded likewise. Whether it was scripted or not, it remains to be seen. The producer may have had his iron claw on these two men because, obviously, the show must go on. Or, was it the need to protect his and Discovery's interest in promoting the show and perpetuate the ongoing myth of Gold Rush? They have contracts with clauses forbidding them to do many things, such as precluding them from joining other broadcasting channels with mining themes or divulging secrets of filming.

It speaks for itself.

Chris and Greg are two fine gentlemen. This is not an opinion, it's a fact. Since I first met Greg after the very first minutes upon arriving at the Sandy Airport auditorium/lodge, he gave me a hearty handshake and a smiling welcome. I first met Chris a few days later and he, like everyone in Todd's crew, tried to squeeze all the blood out of my right hand - I hate to hold onto a wimpy fish-like hand. Chris related the following to me several times:

> "that the show has evolved into a laughing embarrassment with people taking a shot of whiskey every time Todd uses the "F" word, freaking. Whether a group of men at home or at a gathering at a restaurant or saloon, everybody drinks an alcoholic beverage when they hear that expletive being sounded or deleted by Discovery."

Chris told me that he didn't like it when the show was being made into a caricature when groups in bars, restaurants and college dorms exercised excessive indulgence as they collectively saw or heard unbecoming language used by Todd's group. What initially was a prank turned into something that was nothing short of a national embarrassment and excuse for excessive drinking. Although Chris wanted no part in this, he continued to press on.

The following explanations for leaving Todd/Gold Rush were either told personally to me or to another authority: "I left Todd because he cornered me unexpectedly by meeting with everyone in a room demanding my unabashed loyalty in making Gold Rush a continuing success. I said 'yes' but I won't cross the line in lying and misinforming or misleading the TV audience."

Chris told me that sometime later Todd asked him to go into a room with other cast members in attendance. Chris was caught off-guard when Todd cornered him by asking for a full 100% commitment. Not expecting anything out of the this, Todd dropped a bombshell when he confronted Chris by asking, essentially, for his loyalty and devotion. After years of demonstrative dedication and service in Gold Rush and to Todd and every man on the team, Chris asked himself how anyone could even question his dedicated service. Not that he wanted to move on, but he was mystified by all of this and just wanted out.

I knew that this line of questioning really hurt Chris. It's like sacrificing your whole life and well-being for the sake of the mission and then you get stepped on like an ant. But true to his character you will never hear Chris complaining.

Whatever happened to the original theme of men struggling to serve their families by sacrificing themselves on the altar of hard work and esprit de corps?

An incident involving a member of RAW's camera crew who was invited to their morning Bible study in Dave's RV drove the final nail into the coffin. Chris told me that when a RAW film crew member asked the question, in all sincerity:

"Why did Jesus have to die on the cross?"

Todd not only laughed at him but actually ridiculed the RAW questioner. To Chris, this was the pivotal point, the defining moment for him not to remain on the show. Instead of an appropriate, intelligent or even a Scriptural response, Todd responded by jesting him for even asking such a query. To be fair, I know Todd is, without a doubt, a most forthright man, leader, and most importantly, a humble sinner who trusted Christ to be his Savior. I was cordially invited by Todd, et al, to these morning Bible studies which were led by Dave, also a very gracious and generous man. In my opinion, I envisioned that those sequence of events was simply (but regretfully) a quip or clever remark unintentionally made under the wrong circumstances. If we were in that RV with a group of mature believers studying hermeneutics, it would have been understood. Bearing in mind and not making any excuses for anyone, Todd was under extreme pressure working many hours; he literally burned the midnight oil. Under the various responsibilities of leadership, which include planning, logistics, morale, supervision and proficiency, I often work with Todd into the late hours until I saw him falling asleep right before my eyes. I put a blanket on him and quietly left his trailer home. As I have told and written specifically herein, Todd should delegate some responsibility to others in order to give himself more time to rest and mete out his mind. He is trying to execute decisive and proficient leadership while his mind is racing at a million miles a second.

Returning back to the last episode, the "After Show", once Greg and Chris announced their intentions of leaving Gold Rush, whether by design or script, Parker gleefully expresses his need for one or both men to join his work crew. Greg acquiesces to Parker's solicitation while Chris respectfully declined.

Chris announced, professionally and without condemnation so as to not burn any bridges behind him, his intention to leave Gold Rush altogether. No further plans were made other than getting back home and getting on with life and family. Although the money from television was okay and the allotted gold appeared satisfactory, the quest for gold never really diminished. Chris was bitten by the TV bug but not overly enamored by it.

It was not until the mining season was well under way that Chris was asked by a friend to bring him a large machinery piece up to Canada by truck. Upon delivery, he was offered the opportunity to work with Gold Rush again, albeit under new circumstances. One thing led to another and somehow, as we remembered when Parker solicited a general call for help on the third season's last episode, Chris decided to take him up on that offer.

During season one, everyone initially thought that Parker was a boy wonder helping Todd mine gold in Alaska. Nobody's ego was hurt more than Todd's. As a result, Parker's appearance in the show created an allegorical monster akin to what Frankenstein did. Parker's abusiveness and language had become legendary. Even Discovery executives had been on the receiving end. Chris mentored with youths in the greater Oregon area and thought this would be a good opportunity for all parties concerned, especially regarding the executives at Discovery. Later, Chris told me that his presence on Gold Rush, i.e., the fourth season, could be a symbiotic relationship between Parker and himself. Discovery executives definitely thought it was a smart move for Chris to help gauge Parker's outlandish and despotic behavior. It had been reported that Parker's language and disrespect extended to his own parents, a sad commentary but not uncommon in today's devolving society.

Chris is extremely well known by family, friends, Sandy and Oregonians for his generosity of his time and patience in serving his fellow man - truly a consummate professional. Ever since my first introduction of Chris until this present date, I had never heard him utter a word of disunity, disloyalty, or embarrassment to any cause meriting public or private favor. Much like James and Greg, you can put them in your backfield anytime and they'll block for you in getting the football past the goal line without murmur or complaint (ditto the other four).

Looking back at Reagan's first term as president, he once proudly remarked about the courage of our fighting military. He addressed the nation by saying, "Where do we get such men?" Reagan exclaimed it twice, just as Frederic March used it in the closing line of the movie "The Bridges of Toko-Ri" in 1954. I'm confident there are plenty if you only open your eyes and look around. I know I have.

GREG QUITS

According to Wikipedia, provided by a legal representative, it shows the following: "Greg Remsburg, age 41, left the Hoffman crew after season three for undisclosed reasons; however, he returned to work with Parker Schnabel in season four in the Klondike."

Greg was sent home late in the second season for alcoholism reasons. As I arrived at the mine site to further discuss with Todd our plans for the prospective cable channel, he and his crew invited me to join their group photo that I had requested earlier. I asked for the whereabouts of Greg. Todd said that Greg's alcoholism put them at risk and wanted him to clean up his act. No mention was made at that time of whether he would return to Gold Rush. The explanation and filming that Discovery made for Greg's absence at the mine site was his need to seek immediate financial gain to pay bills, thus returning to Sandy, Oregon to find gainful employment; notwithstanding that Greg's wife is a medical/health professional.

Returning back to the third season's last episode, the "After Show", both Greg and Chris announced their intentions to leave Gold Rush. Whether by design or script, Parker expressed his need for one or both men to join his work crew. Greg immediately acquiesced to Parker's solicitation in front of the camera. Since he was an astute businessman with professional experience in several fields, how could he accept an informal, verbal offer of employment without knowing what the requirements were? Undoubtedly not, unless full provisos were previously discussed and agreed upon by all parties concerned.

TRANSPARENCY

Transparency, according to Merriam Webster, is "the quality or state of having the property of transmitting rays of light through its substance so that what is beyond or behind can be distinctly seen".

Today, the word transparency has been used, and aptly so, from one end of the spectrum to the other to refer to equal employment opportunity, fair housing, civil rights and so forth. When used in the context of Gold Rush, one immediately turns to the issue of weighing the amount of gold from each cleanout. Outside opinions have construed the lack of transparency in seeing the actual amount of gold being weighed was an attempt to script the story. Such may be the case as in season one, when Todd needed to find monetary capital to ensure the completion of the mining season in Alaska - that was fulfilled when he borrowed money from his sister.

Dividing up gold nightly

Since no one was present to personally observe and corroborate these measurements, you would have to turn to circumstantial evidence to support your case.

I met with Todd's sister and her husband in one of the annex business offices at the Sandy Airport and found them to be not only amiable but genuinely forthright. I saw nothing to the contrary than what was shown on television. I am referring to the actual incident and not the shooting of it when a camera panned out showing Todd coming into her residence - i.e., camera crew was already in the house filming him coming into the house (meaning it was "scripted").

Secondly, since meeting in Sandy and living with Jack in his RV in Alaska and the Yukon, I have more than a casual acquaintanceship. I have a true personal understanding of who Jack is and what he stands for. He is not only known for being a man of character and genuine sincerity - he would literally give his shirt off his back if you needed help. He demonstrated that character when he was stationed in West Germany, upholding his country's duty during the Soviet Union Cold War. He extended that hand of sincerity for the members of RAW and to everyone in Todd's crew. I have never heard anyone say a negative word or question his character.

At one of our typical breakfast mornings, I noticed Jack was not his usual self. He looked dejected. I asked him what was wrong and he said that "Todd disrespected me in front of the other guys."

I said, "You gotta be kidding."

Jack started to get angry when he told this to me. In doing so, Todd not only disparaged his own father but cut into the very sinew of his own character. Instead of getting into the middle of a family feud, I believed it to be some misunderstanding without any bad intentions. Todd loves his father. Period.

It was not until the show ran its course in the season when I saw how this incident came about. The point here is that it really did happen, but subtly bordered along the line of the sinuous. In other words, wait until after the commercial interruption to find out what happens next, aka cliffhanger. After the show resumes you may see a logical resumption prior to the break or a totally different outcome. That's television massaging (manipulating) a real incident to portray tension. This technique had been used as a mainstay practically by everyone since television's inception. As we know, it backfired when James was used in their cross hairs.

Lastly, in the incident that intimated that James was shown to be the culprit that took gold from the cleanout tent, everyone agreed that that was the lowest point of Discovery's telecast of Gold Rush. This was done solely to hype up/give tension for next week's episode - absolutely nothing whatsoever was shown in the following week during the actual broadcast. Many in the viewing audience found that portrayal of James to be in very poor in taste. There was no follow up nor apology for airing that situation. James told me that was certainly one of the lowest points in his life, "being portrayed as a thief."

While at James' Redmond, Oregon home, he said that whatever gold was found was turned over to Jack for the daily gold measurement. Because of his need to put things and reminders behind him, James gave me his entire share of the first season's gold that was mined in Porcupine Creek. Rather than say James did this out of his need to put Gold Rush behind him and move on with his life, I would instead like to believe that he did that as a result of our friendship. "Or maybe both", I thought.

In fact, I take the responsibility in taking gold that was not added to Jack's daily or 100 ounce total measurement! At that time when I received the gold from Todd that was to be used as business gifts for introducing ourselves to potential qualified investors, there was no thought of how this deficiency would affect the grand season goal of 100 ounces. There was no defalcation of fiduciary responsibility by Jack, neither was there any misappropriation of gold measured, reported or intimated on the show by Todd or any other member of his team. Moreover, transporting unreported/undeclared amounts of gold mined in Canada to the United States would certainly be met by government seizure. It would seem unlikely that Todd (or anyone else) would jeopardize the future of Gold Rush and his television and broadcasting career for just some yellow metal. On a trip back to the Yukon mining site (as previously discussed), I asked Todd for something unique to give to prospective individuals who would be major contributors to our television channel. Instead, of just plain gold or gold mined from the historic Klondike District of the Yukon (by purchasing it from one of several gift shops in Dawson City), it was decided to offer gold personally obtained from the miners of Gold Rush itself. To corroborate this gift of gold I was requesting with Todd's acquiescence, a couple of photos were taken of the vials containing the gold; they were held close to Todd's face.

Therefore (and not realizing at that time), I confess and take responsibility for Todd's missing the second season goal of mining 100 ounces of gold. It was not the fault of anyone on Gold Rush nor was the shortfall due to anyone's neglect of duty. When you add the amount of gold that I was given, it would have added up to reach the second season's goal.

I am responsible for taking the gold and plead guilty. Making James or anyone else a scapegoat for a collective shortfall should not have been the case. In fact, in any leadership role (as Jack had demonstrated in the Army and would agree with me), the man in command should have taken full responsibility for the final outcome of the mission.

In the White House there once was a small placard that sat on the Oval Office desk that read:

"The Buck Stops Here" - Harry Truman.

With respect to the issue of funding the expense of the latest high tech new equipment along with onsite delivery, parts, supplies and fuel, where did the capital come from? Was it internally generated or externally obtained? With less than 100 ounces of gold mined, 10% of that amount paid to the claim owner, plus every team member paid their residual share, that left hardly enough gold (which was not pure, either) to acquire a good second-hand dozer at the Ritchie Bros. auction in Troutdale, Oregon. Unless Todd contacted his stockbroker (?) to buy 1,000 OEX out of the money call options for 1/8 point (totaling $12,500, plus commissions) that went to 30 (totaling $3 million, less commissions), he would have to find new sources of funding the operation.

The only means to fund the full operation of the third season, six months in the northern most of the Yukon, was to use an external source. The question now is whether capital and operational funding was derived from outside investors or the Discovery Channel.

We have already discounted the Texas investor based on my recommendation not to accept his contractual offer. Previous and later episodes have already portrayed potential investors through "dog and pony" solicitation meetings (due diligence). These and other prospective investors were not fully addressed in the show as well. It would have been more than likely that the logical solution of obtaining financing (not only for

Todd, but for Dakota Fred and Parker's full mining operations) would be to obtain a collective lease or purchase agreement from a qualified entity. In addition, let's not forget the value of goods and services obtained in exchange for product placement (Volvo).

Based on the show's portrayal of Parker Schnabel financing the mine through his college savings, the diminutive amount of gold extracted at Porcupine Creek by the Hurts and the anemic gold production by Todd made it appear that funding for the major third season of Gold Rush came as a result of a miraculous financial windfall which landed at their feet (sic Discovery). Remember the old saying:

"Follow the paper trail and, who benefits the most."

HELP

Todd is a very generous man. Here are some examples. When I accompanied him to various locales, especially in Oregon, I witnessed him taking hundreds in cash out of his wallet and giving it to support his friend whose family was in need. In Alaska, he turned the title of a trailer over to a friend who was a pastor of a small but vibrant church; in addition, he also gave him money. Todd and Jack gave their own vital supplies of food and medicine (and vitamins) to complete strangers who were in need at the Alaskan-Canadian border. This was during a period of major economic contraction where men and women had to scrape just to put food on the table.

Todd gave many, many (not stretching his character) items to his team members, including firearms, cold weather gear/clothing and knives. Many gifts were not of small monetary value. To this date, I feel guilty for receiving so much not just from him, but from every member of Todd's Gold Rush team.

With respect to Todd, he gave me many gifts that I did not deserve. When you see his crew working from early morning until late afternoon day in and day out with nothing to contribute by me to the mission or the cause of the show, it's difficult to wonder about his generosity. When I was invited to Greg's RV, I was humbled when I noticed the lack of provisions to sustain his son and himself. As I look back now, I feel bad about receiving gifts not only from Greg but from everyone else there. These unselfish men shared what little they had and gave me their most important possession - their friendship. This is the primary reason for me in lending support to them by returning to the mine site with supplies from the lower 48. I told them that if they ever have any need up there or in South America, that they should contact me and I'll be there very shortly.

DISCOVERY PAYS

Not realizing the amazing success of Gold Rush in its initial inception, Todd was compensated minutely (relatively speaking) by the Discovery Channel. As the season progressed from its launching point from Sandy, Oregon to the finale of its ten episode pilot season, Todd readily recognized its potential and used that to leverage his new found power.

During that time each of the crew (I believe, since I discussed with only some of the crew members) received a $1,000 monthly stipend from Todd. Only the Hoffmans were to be nominally compensated. That all changed during the second season as some of the crew had agents representing their financial interests. Todd lent support by allowing his agent to assist in the salary demand process for the other crew members. Todd told me that in lieu of significantly higher compensation, he would take less in exchange for some control of the show. This became evident (as discussed earlier) in the third season.

It is my understanding that at that time, Todd was to be compensated in the neighborhood of approximately $20,000-28,000 per episode. James, Greg and Chris were compensated in the range of $5,500-8,500 per episode. These figures were contractually secured without direct and full divulgement by every member. Bearing in mind that after Canadian taxes were addressed and after federal, state, and local taxes and other payroll deductions were taken, a token residual was left giving no reason for anyone to happily beat a drum down main street. I almost forgot to mention the big chunk that each agent took right from the top of the check. I won't divulge who described their paychecks as "SLAVE WAGES."

Whether he knew it or not, Todd was about to lose credit of this groundbreaking genre. Another Alaskan type show was about to follow in the same time slot following Gold Rush. That air delivery show lasted one season. When I was in the lower 48, I learned (through my legal/D.C. contacts) that another show featuring a gold mining theme was about to be launched in Alaska. In my effort to notify Todd upon discovering this revelation, I was unable to contact him at that time since his cell phone number that he gave me no longer worked. I had names of the individuals who were just fabricating the concept of today's hit "Bering Sea Gold."

Whether by design or coincidence, I am sure it made an indelible impression on Todd's psyche that this creative concept was kidnapped and is still being usurped not only by Discovery executives, but by other cable channels as well. There are literally dozens of shows that spun off of Todd's initial concept. It is like having Mary Wollstonecraft Shelley's famous creation turned the great Boris Karloff's depiction of the monster in "Frankenstein" into "Abbott & Costello Meet Frankenstein", "Young Frankenstein" and, finally, television's "The Munsters". You get the idea.

As the seasons progressed with the phenomenal success of Parker's surpassing not only his but Todd's personal gold extraction targets, one would certainly believe that Todd would become resentful and jealous.

Before discussing this any further, let's give credit where credit is due. First, it takes excellent business acumen to run a gold mining operation like Parker's. Second, it takes leadership to be technically and tactically proficient. By selecting the right men (personnel) and looking out for their welfare, it will ensure the mission is understood, supervised and accomplished. Making sound and timely decisions is exemplary, especially in an environment hostile to those accustomed in the lower 48 states. One would not have difficulty imagining the influence and impact Parker would offer in selecting other endeavors of his choice. You have already heard and would heartily agree that Parker is "wise beyond his years."

On a side note again (if you don't mind), I complemented Parker to his grandfather when I first bumped into John Schnabel as he was moving earth in widening that narrow road that led into the Porcupine Creek mine site. I recognized him of course as he was perched in the cab of a giant dozer. We exchanged pleasantries. It is easy to see why John Schnabel is so beloved by Parker, his family, friends and the worldwide audience. [I just learned today of Messr. Schnabel's graduation into glory. While we reminisce his words, smile, love and friendship, it won't be that long until we meet with him again to renew our fellowship.]

Since I really believe Todd shares my same observation and sentiment of Parker as a successful businessman and leader, there would be less thought of jealousy and more inclination towards the line of a friendly rivalry. You have seen Todd reacting this way in front of the camera; based upon personal observations of him, he personified that off camera as well. Competition in of itself, like sports, will only make you a better person with better results. In the case of gold mining, it's the (financial) bottom line. Therefore, the only contentious feeling, if any, is with Discovery's usurping of a genre that was started by Todd.

In the realm of jurisprudence, you cannot copyright nor patent a general, nonexclusive concept.

FINDING GOLD

"Just when they began to see gold, they lost their claim."

Not knowing the Hoffmans until the conclusion of its inaugural season, my impression of vacating Porcupine Creek was certainly in the cards, as they say in a strictly colloquial sense. That is, Todd already knew he was not going to mine in Alaska again, at least not at Earl Foster's Porcupine Creek. He told me that the lease owner did not tell the truth about the amount or level of proven or unproven gold that was supposed to be estimated there, based on testing or past precedence. Without being libelous, Todd may have inferred to have stated that the prospect of producing gold could have been exaggerated.

By this time, Todd already knew they were not going to mine significantly in the same Alaskan site and so decided to relocate to the Yukon. He planned to be in the Yukon. Wayne Fisher's roadside wash plant had been contracted for purchase. He just had to play it out for TV/Discovery's audience.

Of course this could mean that the success of extracting gold would be based upon the experience of the workers as well as having the appropriate equipment, fuel and supplies for such an endeavor. Mining is not an exact science. Even with the best technology and variables on your side, you could miss the entire vein by an inch. Besides, the Hurts did succeed in extracting gold from that mining claim that was vacated by the Hoffmans. The question of eviction depends on who the respondents are. The Schnabel claim across the nearby creek/river has been a successful mining site for years. Todd told me about the issue of the water levels needed for mining at Porcupine. While we were all fulfilling the administrative classes in mining regulations and testing at a local Haines high school classroom, Todd told me that the water levels were insufficient per regulatory requirements.

It was clearly noted in an "After Season" episode that the Hoffmans traveled to the Yukon to seek alternative mining claims to Alaska. The only preemption to the mining site in Yukon was the attempted restart of draining and digging the glory hole site from season one. Without the intent of actually mining there, Todd chose this as a tactical retreat to absolve his obligation(s) in Alaska and proceeded onward to the Yukon.

Upon arrival in Dawson City, Todd continued to seek a mining claim by making telephone inquiries from a public phone down from the central main street. This was only done since he hadn't had his internet set up yet. Todd stayed up till the wee hours of night making inquiries. He said that he usually tried to connect with individuals who were also like-minded in terms of his Christian faith. He wanted to collaborate with individuals willing to sacrifice to a higher cause and who were not monetarily motivated. By finding the right individual(s) to providing the right mining claims, he would be able to captivate a television audience for a second season. Therefore, Todd's premise of successive, incremental gold yield would be achieved and shown exploitatively. In year one, 10 ounces. In year two, 100 ounces and in year three, 1,000 ounces.

To ensure continued high TV ratings, the cycle must be repeated. Season four would be a throwaway gold production year. The fifth would be the new base year, followed by increased success in the sixth season, and ending in exaggerated success for the last season, thereby becoming eligible for syndication. As we know, the fourth year was a diversion or a throw away season to be followed by the tested and proven grounds of the

Yukon. As discussed, the financial expense of moving an entirely new mining operation several thousands of miles away to a different continent costs an enormity beyond an ordinary, average/typical budget; it would be quite ludicrous. I would question the mindset of any external investor who would look at an investment with mediocre performance and short-term history.

The inherent risk in a declining value of a commodity like gold has made it lose its luster. In defense of the Hoffmans, I was offered in more than one instance to purchase the Sandy Airport - lock, stock and barrel. What would I need with an airport since I don't know how to fly single-engine experimental aircraft (landing strip not long enough to handle a 787 down to a single-engine fixed wing)? Kato had piloted single-engine Cessnas to a U.S. Air Force twin-engine training jet [and also the lead engine of a central Paris subway train (I was invited by the engineer)].

Given the stalwart persistence of Todd or due to the large carrots held in front of him, he was able to secure mining claims in the Yukon region to carry out the show for another season. This obviously was not the typical way of gold mining for the average prospector unless you have the backing of a major cable channel behind you.

QUIPS

Jack: "You're all millionaires, the only thing is you have to get it out of the ground."

Todd: "You're about to lose your house. You're bankrupt."

Todd: "As a leader you have to take the responsibility for all your actions and the blame - you take your lumps."

Jack: "I'm a man of action, not so much words."

Fred: "I've been married for 35 years, to three different women."

Kato: "The need to document is parole evidence. The more elaborate, the more it can be backed up. Faked phone calls between Todd ...demonstrate less credibility."

Kato: "It's not how fast you drive, it's how you drive fast."

Kato: "You're not ready to live until you're ready to die."

> "Look! We're rich! We're millionaires."

From Chaplin's "The Gold Rush"

WHY ME?

An instance occurred when we parked our RVs in Haines, Alaska. It was an area with electrical and water hookups and a few motel-type rooms. I was installing the toilet flexi-hoses from the RVs to the sewage pipes. Thinking nothing of it, Todd and Jack remarked that it was a humbling experience. To me, it was a necessity that someone had to do. That was it. However, they called it a turning point for which they wanted me to be in their cast. I said (what else, of course):

"You gotta be kidding."

This was not their last request for me to be a cast member in front of the camera.

Somehow, word spread that I would be favorable as a personality in the show and it made its way to Chris. I had never mentioned the Hoffmans' invitation but Chris chided me thinking my presence in the show would be timid, to say the least. He demonstrated the methodology of talking to the television audience through the camera as a second party person.

Chris said something along this line: "Kato, listen to me as I am explaining: pretend you're talking to a person instead of a camera filming you...this tool I'm holding will turn off the water flow really quick...you got it, Kato?"

I replied "You gotta be kidding."

I've been interviewed on national TV, debated with the Vice President on C-SPAN, appeared in "The Streets of San Francisco" - Karl Malden & Michael Douglas, local television and on radio, and appeared on a couple of movies like Clint Eastwood's last Dirty Harry movie saga, "The Dead Pool". Me bashful?

Being pressed again, I said why? "I don't benefit; there's no consideration involved nor do I want or need it."

It was to benefit the show and His mission, Jack said. Jack thought that I was a private individual who relished his privacy. I concur to a certain point. Todd's crew even speculated as to the reason why I refused. My actions later quickly dispelled any such notions.

Questions that were raised by Discovery representatives included whether my intentions were sincere or not. In several instances, most of them embarrassing ones, Discovery representatives kept hounding me and the Hoffmans so that I would sign standard non-disclosure forms and waivers. I acquiesced in every instance, but up to a point. I signed practically everything that they stuck in front of my nose and they still wanted more. In a couple of instances, RAW was trying to find a niche that I could fill or a role that would explain my presence on the show. They asked about my professional work experience, education and life in the not too distant past. It got to the point of ridiculousness that my standard diatribe was:

> "I was peeling potatoes at McDonalds when Jack saw me as he was having his usual Saturday morning breakfast with his buddies."

They instantly knew that response wasn't believable nor would it hold water, as they might say. I was told later that McDonalds used packaged, pre-cut potato fries delivered to each restaurant. Jack chuckled. He knew what KP duty was. When Discovery pressed further, I standardized my response by borrowing a line you always hear from every Cabinet member appointed by the President: "I serve at the pleasure of the Pres........ Hoffmans."

Bottom line: "There is nothing to be gained in knowing people and allowing myself to be known by them."

In essence, Todd wanted me to fill a void in the show's storyline for an (external/outside) investor.

James, on the other hand, was somewhat supportive of my position. I, as well as the overwhelming audience of Gold Rush, believed that if James had something to say, he would say it, but not without hesitation in thinking of what and how to say it. He knew my position as well as Todd's mission of the show and was adamant in agreeing with me that I should be a supporter behind the camera and not in front of it.

Except for Todd, no one knew at that time of my role in advising him on financial and legal issues, personally and business-wise. While we were partners on the BATTLEGROUND series project, we were looking ahead. I said that there must be life even after Gold Rush, and that included other shows planned for exploitation. We had a code(word) that we used that entailed future programming leading to ownership of a television channel [saving it for later]. A primary consideration of course, was control. An example for the need of control is editing. Todd and most, if not all of his crew, had a very objectionable stance towards the formal or fictitious censoring adopted by Discovery for the use of expletives. For the sake of ratings, expletives spoken or inferred by censor gave a very negative impression and connotation at the expense of moral convictions.

An important area of discussion about my role in the show was based upon my experience as an analyst. Watching the first season and experiencing it in the second season, I prepared memos (serving as parole evidence) to improve time management, cost effectiveness and system efficiency.

I didn't realize until much later that Todd was getting advice from both sides, from James and myself. As discussed previously, and to reiterate - James only wanted to be an adviser and not a person capable of physically working for any significant lengths of time. James told me that Dave is replacing him as the team's technical adviser as time elapsed on the show. His list of recommendations was cordially received by Todd but was not fully implemented.

Recognizing that mistakes, "accidents" and shortfalls made for better TV (and ratings) than a smoothly operating, fine-tuned machine, James saw no future need of his professional services and resigned. He was not fired as the show had suggested. Again, the need for ratings prevailed over reality with the appearance of James' dismissal by Todd.

WHERE'S THE BEEF?

Bargaining with salaries:
I was told by Todd that he could have insisted and should have received higher salaries (at least for him and his father) but he took less in exchange for more editing control. If not for editing control, he could have held out for equipment needed for the mining operation. In this way, there would be no need for real "investors".

Internal: If Todd mined <10 oz. in season one, then there would be virtually no money left for him to finance season two. The quality of gold produced at Porcupine Creek was not very pure – I have Harness' gold to prove that.

In season two, it was reported in the show that less than 100 oz. was produced. Using optimistic figures and rounding up: $1,700/oz. X 100 oz. = $170,000.

With Todd, Greg, Chris and James' gold tested for purity in San Francisco by two different companies, we arrived at a value of approximately $750-950/oz.; adjusting for the price of gold when it was higher, the value would have been $850-1,100/oz. Assuming that everyone was paid the same rate of 5 oz. as James was then the additional amounts of Greg, Chris, Jim and Dave's would have totaled approximately 25 oz., leaving about 75 oz. Optimistically, the value of Todd and Jack's gold would be:$750/oz. X 75 oz.=$56, 250 to $1,100/oz. X 75oz.=$82,500. These amounts would hardly finance the entire operation of season three for Todd. Other sources of internal funding include cash contributed by companies to place products in the show. Lastly, season two could also have been financed with the Hoffman paychecks from season one and two. In addition, their own personal funds could have been tapped as well. The logical progression could be that there was more gold produced but not revealed to the crew members or television audience. Budgeting the revelation of gold produced can fit that bill.

External: As the worldwide appetite of gold reached $1,700 an ounce, I warned Todd representing or fronting a third party selling a commodity that could fall precipitously in price, thereby inviting lawsuits from disgruntled investors. Having to backtrack a commitment that was already filmed with the Texas gold bullion company (that included unreal staging at the Sandy Airport), Discovery had to fund the void and provide financing for Todd's group. The executives of the Discovery Channel obviously had the greatest interest in continuing Gold Rush's high ratings. By leveraging equipment, fuel and supplies from major companies (including product placement, e.g., Volvo), Discovery could have easily financed or outright funded Todd, Parker and the Hurts for the third season.

Individual investors lacked the ability to perform due diligence to finance the Hoffman's mining operation. No major mining company, public or private, would want to invest, finance or joint venture with any of the Hoffman mining operations without approval of shareholders or partners based on Todd's past/unproven performance. ANYONE executing superficial due diligence would recognize that the venture of gold mining conducted on a very small scale would provide limited returns risking total loss.

JAMES HARNESS - IN HIS OWN WORDS

"I had tried to save a failing business that I had started. It got to where I couldn't even work, my pain levels were so high. I had no doctors, no medication. And I just folded."

"All the walls came crashing in and I was down to nothing. I was on my last legs. Didn't have a lot of money. I had applied for disability. I was mainly doing stuff for the Hoffmans just to have a place to stay. And when they came up with this other deal, going gold mining. Because they knew I was down and out, they offered it to me, 'Can you build this stuff?'"

In a Gold Rush episode entitled "Revelations" it depicted James' departure from the show. James saw the sneak peeks intimating his exit and was disquieted with the show's depiction of him.

"It insinuated that Todd fired me, which never happened. It shows him (Todd) making a comment that 'I guess this is where we part ways.' Yet I'm not in the frame. I'm not there. It truly is not the way I remember it, and it distorts my memories...I get mad, because it's different from what I remember. The real important things I feel should have been in there weren't. For every forty hours of filming, you might see two minutes of it. And sometimes it's what you leave out that's important. I don't care if it's falling down or killing yourself, they want to see it again and get two shots of it... It's really hard to have a competitive business and put everything into that - trying to make a profit you built out of the ground - and yet try to do a TV show at the same time. They collide constantly. It slows you down so much, there's no way to succeed. You're doing two different things at the same time."

"The definition of insanity is doing the same thing over and over again and expecting different results."

Gold Rush: "It was a job."
Being recognized: "but it actually grows on you. It's flattering, a little bit..." "it is crazy."

"It's pretty crazy. And when you go looking for it, it never seems to happen. Probably the worst one so far was the Houston airport. I got off the plane and it was a long ways, like a quarter of a mile to the next stop to get on a plane. And that's a big airport. So I got on one of those 12-seat golf carts, and the (driver) wouldn't take off until it was full. People started to recognize me, so they're bringing over purses and business cards, anything they can to get me to sign them and stuff. And then the girl takes off. So I got, like 15 people chasing me through the airport, trying to get their stuff back. That was the funniest."

"I've had people follow me around and do double takes. One guy followed me from one corner of Walmart clear to the other, when I went to get the cat liter. They get pretty excited sometimes. They say 'How's your back?' 'How're you doing?' 'What are you doing here?' "

Gold Rush: "But not everywhere. Usually it's confined to one type of music or one area. When they started (airing) in 172 countries, it's pretty hard to go somewhere and not have people know who you are."

Self-described hero: "It's scary sometimes, because you don't know what they're going to put. It could incriminate you the rest of your life. I have never been (a bad guy). I've always been the hero. And I'm sorry to say most think (the show) has turned into one. This disappoints me to almost tears after all I have done for everyone. It only shows me that I am right not to trust show business to be fact. It's only entertainment, not to be taken seriously."

Resigned: "I guess the only way to stay sane and look at this is I am a paid actor doing a part in a show, and if they choose to make me a bad guy in he part they can edit that way . . . sure makes me have a wake-up call on the fact that it's only entertainment and so far from reality."

20/20 hindsight or Monday morning quarterbacking on going to Alaska: "NO"

"I don't think it was even about the gold. If it falls out of the sky or hit somebody in the head, great. I'm sure anybody would welcome that, but was it business to have a TV show or was it a mine to mine gold? How could it be both? There's no room for both."

Regarding his departure from Gold Rush: "I am finished, my health's not the greatest. Once you're blessed with chronic pain, you have to reorganize your life and how you do things."

Regarding the season finale portraying him as a thief: "The word is they will write me off the show somehow, try to show me in a bad light. As I was afraid of, I was badly represented, with post-fabricated and altered facts. They were conveniently put into place to alter their meaning and benefit an alternate storyline chosen to discredit me."

"Gold Rush='Deadliest Catch' put on land."

"It was a struggle to get gold out of the ground, struggle with nature, each other, bears."

Cameramen: "were pushy about what they wanted to get, even if it was not what you would have done in a normal day. They might do forty hours of filming and you might see two minutes or less."

"Profits from the show subsidized the miners for the first year."

At first, "the show was secondary to the mining, or so I was led to believe. It was interesting for me to watch how the show evolved; it's been a big hit. We never expected it to be a huge success."

Regarding recognition: "Walmart, any store I go into, people know who I am."

Regarding music: "I have the capability to do all kinds of crazy things. Making choices is the hard part."

As a last resort: "There's always stuff to fix."

I asked James many unanswered questions that I (and most viewers) wanted to know. Many of these "Q&A" sessions were not in the least bit done on a formal basis. These talks, discussions or exchanges were done on motorcycles, eating out in nice restaurants, or "racing" down Walmart aisles while buying food and supplies. Here are a couple more examples:

To stay or leave: James had to choose between temporarily leaving the show and visiting his mother, or help the show by staying? Not knowing the severity of her illness, he chose to stay, and so James' mother passed on without him at her bedside. Needless to say, James was devastated. Fortunately, James was consoled with the prayers and support of Todd's men. He made it through.

"I will always be thankful and indebted to my fans and the Gold Rush guys for their support in seeing me through. This had been a most difficult period in my life", he told me one evening while waiting for dinner to be served.

After James left the show, he told me face to face that he gave Todd a list of recommendations for improving the success of the mine's operation. This was done before or at the beginning of the second season. Without a firm reply, James acquiesced and went up to Alaska again. Ultimately, James did not receive acknowledgment of these suggestions so he left – he was not fired for poor performance or for "stealing gold", as Discovery had portrayed him in the following week's promo. Todd must have known these recommendations were real. However, success and smoothness sometimes could be boring or lack the TV suspense that failure would provide. Oftentimes, there is more action and interest in human and mechanical failure.

"Where's the gold you promised?" as James asked Todd. After the season's end, not everyone was getting their cut of the gold. I cannot speak for everyone, but James told me that for whatever reason, Todd did not want to give him his share of the gold. Upon James' "mild" insistence (my humor of using this level of compelling), Todd relented and yielded to James' demand that he should get his cut of the gold.

Considered by many as the real hero of the show, James sacrificed his body, mind and spirit for the success of the show until his body finally gave out.

"With Todd and Jack, and to some extent Jim, I saw these guys take a back seat when shooting demands their appearance and then returning back to their trailers when the camera is turned off." At first I smiled and then laughed with James when he was the first one ever to use this terminology, "Gone Hollywood."

Music: Initially unaware of his other talents, I quickly learned of James' musical ability when I rode up with him to Alaska and the Yukon. We listened to some of his compositions and bands that he played in. He played the drums for me at the airport but without accompaniment and even then, it sounded pretty good. James wanted to put together his own band and tour the country while writing and recording. I already observed him warehousing sound equipment and other musical instruments, first at Sandy and then more completely in Redmond. We seriously discussed the financial requirements needed to assemble a new band. With much anticipation, we continued with this dialogue even to his last days. Anyone could recognize that James knew that "the sky's the limit."

QUARTERMASTER GENERAL

Before leaving with Todd and his group, I prepared for my trip by bringing significant supplies the group would need. This included medical/first aid and intermediate care items (I prepared notification and emergency first-responder packets), health and hygiene items, dozens of cases of GNC vitamins and supplements, scores of cases of canned and dried fruit, enriched juices, energy bars and cookies, snacks, canned meat, pasta, water purification systems and filters, solar-powered lamps, solar-heated portable showers, etc. On a separate mid-season supply run, I included similar items as mentioned above. One different item stood out-cologne. When I discharged a squirt, Chris said in his usual jovial humor, "stop spraying that rat urine (p___) on me." We laughed.

All items and supplies were purchased for the mutual benefit of everyone and success for the accomplishment of the mission. I remembered one of the favorite items RAW enjoyed was Sam Maynard's "Mr. Brown Coffee".

Through the major efforts of Mike Fox, who also resided at Sandy Airport, Todd received significant amounts of products via endorsements and placements on Gold Rush. This included .50 caliber pistols from Magnum Research, whose sales increased exponentially, Arctic Cat ATVs, cold weather gear, mosquito repellent products, caps, gloves, high intensity headlamps and so forth. More companies were solicited each season: they paid Todd generously for the opportunity to have their merchandise appear on the show. Jim gave Kato some cold weather gear (Wright & McGill Co.- jacket and pants) in the Yukon. I thanked him and Todd, et al., and thought that was nice of them to think of me.

While having dinner with Chris after the season finale, I learned that each of Todd's crew got the same Wright & McGill cold weather gear except him. I remarked that I got a set given to me as a thank you gift from Jim. Obviously, it was supposed to have been given to Chris, which he never got.

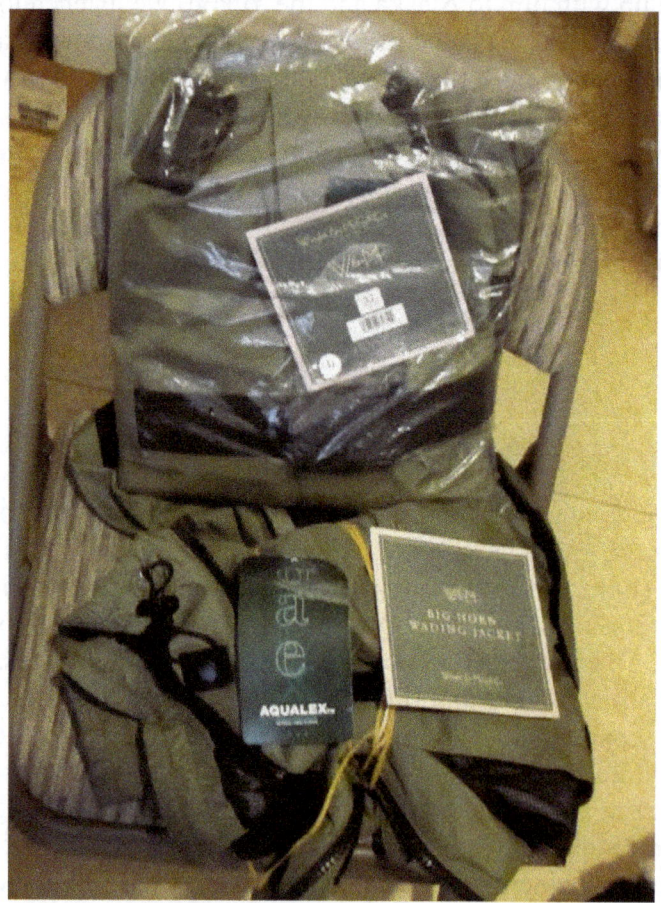

Jim's gift of Chris' gear to Kato

I said, "That must have been your set that you should have been given to be worn and shown on TV as a product placement or some other promotion."

Chris says, "Oh, well, that's the way it goes."

I said, "Chris, do you want it now?"

Chris says, "No, it's alright. You keep it, Kato."

I felt bad not knowing that Chris didn't share in the bounty (booty). I offered Chris that unopened gear because Kato is thick skinned and didn't need cold weather protection. While he declined to take it, I knew Chris was hurt. Chris says Thurb is the quartermaster general (Kato's word definition) for Todd.

In bringing boxes of cold weather gear and many other items on one of the supply trips I made by myself, I felt really bad to have received something that was essential to the need and efficiency of one of the crew members. It is hoped that this was just an oversight made by Jim and nothing more of it. It was noted that Jim's "hogging of items" (not my words but a quote from someone else) did not end there, as I was told. I choose not to mention any more of this matter since it serves no purpose except promote divisiveness. However, you have to remember that Jim was instrumental in organizing and deploying the materiel needed for critical use in adverse environments. As an experienced, professional hunter and sportsman, it's no wonder that Jim was designated by Todd as "Quartermaster General" for carrying out this important responsibility.

With respect to Arctic Cat off-road vehicles and other large items provided by manufacturers for promotion and stored at the airport, I do not know what became of them since they may have been used to film future seasons.

TOP TEN LIST (OF RISKS

Listed in increasing threat levels are instances of physical risk during this Alaskan-Canadian venture:

10+Confronting someone entering Todd's RV.

9+Driving Jim Thurber's truck that fell into roadside-shoulder ice.

8+Maneuvering a wayward Sturgeon.

7+Stranded and walking alone in the wild.

6+Stopping a theft at night.

5+Chasing a thief.

4+Bear hunting alone in Alaska.

3+Bear hunting with no bullets.

2+Home invasion.

And as David Letterman so often said on "The Late Night Show", "Rounding the top ten list":

1+Napoleon Dynamite.

COMMENTARY ON THE TOP 10 LIST

10+From inside the auditorium-lodge where I was staying as their guest, I watched 360 degrees through several large windows for any movement. A little past midnight, I saw a shadow coming towards Todd's RV beyond the hangars. Based upon my experience, I left the building, circled around, approached the individual from behind, and lit "him" up with my high beam Maglite. To my astonishment and the subject's surprise, Mrs. Todd Hoffman nearly dropped all of the boxes she was carrying. I asked what was going on and she said, "I'm bringing these boxes of food for me to eat up there." I helped her stow these diet/nutritional victuals in a storage compartment. Conclusion: The prima facie evidence presumes that wives, at least one, were to go up to the mine site during the filming of the show. Monetary compensation could also play a part for this strategy.

9+While making a 3-point turn in a narrow street off the main thoroughfare with Jim's newly acquired dually, I reversed into a black ice trough or channel that tipped the truck 45 degrees. How embarrassing. After a mile or so hike, I found a very cordial heavy equipment operator who extricated the truck by lifting it out with his dozer. This Alaskan gentleman refused my monetary offer of gratitude. I breathed a sigh of relief to myself saying, "Another typical (gracious) Alaskan."

8+Needing to get back home ASAP, both Jack and Todd allowed me to drive the Sturgeon SUV to California. Jack, through no small effort of his own, got documentation that allowed me to drive it through Canada and the U.S. - this included title, registration and insurance. Although I got there late, the Sturgeon got me where I wanted. After the funeral, I returned to Sandy to load up the Sturgeon with supplies needed for Todd's crew. About half way through Washington, I noticed that the Sturgeon's steering was beginning to have extra "play", i.e., excessive over steering. It became more pronounced while driving through British Columbia. As I was driving from one side of the narrow two-lane gravel road to the other (while under 30 mph) I couldn't hold the vehicle in my lane. The Surgeon went into the ditch to the right at about 10 mph.

7+Without any wheels or anyone else on the deserted road, I left the village and walked for hours in the light rain. I wasn't too worried about food or water, nor buffalo, giant elk or moose. On my maiden drive with the Sturgeon back to California, I saw something out of the ordinary, the largest grizzly bear on the planet. I hoped to not meet with it again as I trekked on foot, since I only had my Buck knife for protection. I was rescued by a cordial Canadian who took me to a small truck stop at least a hundred miles away.

6+As everyone was already bedded down for the night while on our way up to Alaska, I observed a pickup truck with two male occupants cruising around a restaurant parking lot. It did the same in a hotel parking lot, looking and stopping at different intervals. Upon leaving that parking area, the vehicle approached one of our RVs and stopped alongside to look in the back of the truck. I casually but hastily jogged across the street and approached them from the rear on the right side and lit them up on their passenger side with my Maglite. They quickly took off without further incidence.

5+Late at night at the Gold Rush RV campsite in Dawson City, I observed from inside Jack's RV a WMA (white male) - he was rummaging through the back of trucks. As the subject arrived at the back of Jim's truck, he started to take some tools. So I got out of Jack's RV and nonchalantly approached him so I can collar him. He dropped what he was taking and took off like a jack rabbit being chased by a coyote. I gave a verbal warning to stop (like he'll obey) and took off after him. (This obviously took place before my leg injury at the Fishers' property). After seeing him high hurdle a fence without breaking a stride, I thought the better part of valor would be to return to the RV park empty handed.

4+With a valid bear tag and hunting license, I tried to acquire an ample supply of caloric protein to sustain the crew members for at least a couple of weeks. I remember that in season one, they enjoyed cuisine along the likes of "bearittos" (their words, not mine). At the 33 Mile Roadhouse restaurant outside Haines' city limits, they informed me of bear sightings a day or two before. With that intel, I hiked along and across the river (knee high at the shallowest crossing) to the road where I first met Messr. John Schnabel on his dozer and looked for more recent bear tracks. Unsuccessful up until that point, I returned the next day in Jim's truck and waited in concealment and downwind for two days without any bear sightings. I returned to Todd's caravan and was surprised to learn that they were a little more than mildly concerned for my whereabouts for the last couple of days. In reality, I think Jim needed his wheels back.

3+After spending an exciting and gratifying day hunting bear with men from the Wounded Warrior program in Alaska, I wanted to hunt bear by myself early before dawn. With about a pound of salmon left over from dinner (the best!), I left the good accommodations they provided us and proceeded to look for a favorable spot to wait. After a short while, I opened the .50 caliber revolver they provided me and my mouth dropped when I saw it was empty. It was fully loaded the night before. I quickly picked up my salmon "sampler" and ran back to the cabin just to find them grimacing. They were laughing at me holding those cartridges in his hand to see if I came back with bear claws etched into my face. Because of my usual stoic countenance, I think they wanted me to return to Canada's Yukon a little bit more melodramatic.

2+On my usual self-imposed night watch, in this instance about an hour before dawn at the Gold Rush RV campground in Dawson City, I noticed a male behind the main office building walking between various RVs. This individual was making a double beeline straight to Jack's door. I grabbed Jack's 12 gauge pump shotgun, racked a round which awakened Blue, released the safety and waited for the subject's next move. The man grasped the door handle and broke the plane separating the realm of the public domain and the closed quarters of a private residence. In a quick nanosecond, I had to postulate the repercussions of discharging the weapon from my position in the RV. Because of the choke, some of the nine 00 buck shots could have easily penetrated Jack's closed bedroom door and would have severely injured or even kill him in his room to the rear. Since I had no opportunity to re-position myself for the trajectory of the buckshot that would be away from the rear where Jack was sleeping, I instead directed loud and distinct commands to the intruder,

"STOP...GET OUT...TURN AROUND...DROP TO YOUR KNEES...
CLASP YOUR FINGERS BEHIND YOUR HEAD"

I grabbed his interlocked fingers with my left hand, pushed him down prostrated, place my left knee to his lower back, laid the shotgun down flat outside the subject's reach, patted him down for weapons with my emptied hand, ordered him to stand down while pointing the shotgun back at his head and contacted the RCMP. I advised the authorities on the phone that the subject posed no further threats and was cooperating.

Royal Canadian Mounted Police shoulder patch

1+To date, it still baffles my mind and remains a mystery as to why Todd watches the "Napoleon Dynamite" DVD so frequently. Unless someone shares the similar talents of Spock's (the late Leonard Nimoy) mind meld, I can only speculate here since no one can probe into someone's mind and render motive and/or judgment without prejudice or preconceptions. Todd shared snacks and watched this DVD with some of his crew members in his spacious RV. Upon watching this movie for the first time I "discovered" how simplistic the storyline was as well as learned of its low production cost. I also learned from Todd that it was a huge success in terms of its gross theatrical receipts, pay per view and video/DVD sales; a figure well over $100 million. If my memory serves me correct, I was told that this film was made by the Mormons. I still don't understand the significance of who produced this film. I qualified the foregoing remarks by saying that this movie can be construed as a harbinger of success for (sic) Gold Rush/Todd Hoffman, et al.

LIFE AFTER

Because Chris and Greg are still shooting Gold Rush, and are thus forbidden under contractual agreement precluding them to work in similar mining type shows in different competing channels, divulging copyright materials, and prohibited from entertaining and accepting television offers within a reasonable amount of time upon leaving Gold Rush, they are each bound not to publish or assist in such matters of dissemination until contractual obligation terminates or lapses. With the passing of James Harness and the period of nearly two years after leaving the show, it no longer holds him accountable for any promulgation of facts and opinions formed during his tenure with Gold Rush. Therefore, these statements from James were obtained freely without coercion, obligation or due compensation in 2013 and 2014, personally and by telephone.

With his public recognition as being one of the original leading cast members of a ground-breaking show that is still currently broadcasted, it was difficult for James to put it totally behind him. We have spoken a lot of times about this but only in passing and not at the point of conversation. It's not really hard to explain this.

You know when a man who likes talking to a man who likes to talk, they are a breed apart. If you are really acquainted with someone, you can not only trust but share some of the most intimate, personal and important things without reservations whatsoever – you have something far more rare and valuable than a 1,000 ounce gold nugget. To date, I cannot even count on one hand the number of people I can speak freely and openly as I had with James. In conversations we have had, he shared information that I will never divulge and will carry to my grave. It's not like emails or private texts immediately made by presidential candidate Hillary Clinton during her tenure as Secretary of State in the tragic Benghazi, Libya attack in 2012; these were topics and matters relevant to the individual and those whom he cares for.

Because of the number of wars and conflicts our country has had (not only in the 21st century, but even since Vietnam and Korea), we may personally know of men and women who sacrificed their life and limbs in the defense and service of their country. There are hundreds of thousands in VA hospitals and retirement homes living each day in physical and mental pain. Today we recognize PTSD (post traumatic stress disorder) as serious, if not more than some physical injuries incurred on the battlefields. James had to face injuries that were permanent and wide in scope. You have to not only be mentally strong to overcome your physical injuries but maintain strength in mind to sustain yourself each day. When your physical body is asked to perform way beyond its current capabilities, the mind is going to be taxed far more. The mindset is compounded even more when your private life becomes an open book read by millions each week. And, obviously, when your persona is amplified by being an unsung hero, the weight of responsibility (whether real or not) is nevertheless placed on your back - you have to carry it off screen as well. We have read many stories of those in the public eye succumbing to such heavy burdens.

Fortunately, James Harness did not succumb but actually flourished. You may have already read accounts from his other friends who knew him well too. His abilities beyond engineering and electronic fields included music composition and performance. While riding up to Alaska and Canada, we listened to all kinds of music, including those he wrote and performed in bands. James wanted to organize and head his own band but that required capital. It was not easy, but it was not impossible to form his own hard rock band. To achieve this, I asked if he would be interested in helping me as a partner to create other television shows for our own channel. Forming a television channel was relatively easy - content was the problem. I told James that we needed shows that other stations would never be able to broadcast - shows that men and women would want to see and not have our I.Q.'s being taken for granted by watching.

Although I created about one hundred treatments at the Sandy Airport auditorium one (long) night, I felt that most of them should be short lived and not run for more than two seasons, three at the most. We would not be interested in filming or broadcasting episodes for the sake of syndication. Audience interest will gauge our performance. James liked my ideas and felt the concept of one shot filming is what reality TV should be. In other words, no retakes.

James' ideas for future television programming included an Australian opal mining expedition, to which he already made contacts in Sydney, an Oregon gold mining operation, possible Fisher property gold mining, proprietary automobile and motorcycle customizing, electronic-fiber optics development and logistical consultant to African and South American ventures. In other words, he had a lot on his plate. As a matter of personal honor, we had a gentleman's agreement on literally everything we dealt in. I didn't need a written contract from James because he always delivered--his words were as good as gold (no pun intended). As the saying goes, very rarely do you bump into someone who can deliver the goods they promised on a hand shake. After seeing what he had already accomplished, I see absolutely no reason why James could not have fulfilled his dreams, given the necessary resources.

However, there were two nemeses in his life. I really shouldn't say his physicality was one of them. He was aware of his vertebrae condition and other injuries he suffered throughout his life, he never used them as an excuse to not meet his obligations. I accompanied James to physicians and hospitals in Oregon and never heard him complain once (except for year+ old magazines and journals in the waiting room). Despite what we saw on Gold Rush regarding James getting pain relief in an East Coast medical facility, it was not permanent but just temporary. James acquiesced to my request of going to the Stanford Medical Center in the Bay Area, the vanguard of the medical field as far as I was concerned. I've been there myself on a couple of occasions. I walk the talk by bringing Chris there as well. I offered Jack the same opportunity to get the best medical attention in the world at Stanford. James was pleased with the opportunity of getting relief of chronic pain.

The other nemesis in his life was the IRS. Failing to meet his financial obligation in paying his payroll taxes in a timely fashion was a problem that almost consumed his total well-being. James was constantly afraid of having his personal property confiscated/seized or disability payments garnished to satisfy his indebtedness. He told me that he was afraid of leaving his place of residence (where he was a leasehold tenant) unattended for long periods of time, i.e., hours. It was not a paranoia of any sort but a material possibility that would violate his personal well-being. In addition, tantamount to an uninvited intrusion, James has had trespassers on his property, including one that broke into the rear of the house by the hot tub room. On my last trip to visit James, we had planned to reinforce the security perimeter, the house and the other buildings and structures on the property. I wasn't going to personally install anything but wanted to observe James implement those security circles firsthand so that I could learn from him. Unfortunately, it was not to be. As far as James told me, he was successful in having his indebtedness to be repaid in accommodating, scheduled payments.

In conclusion, James wanted to stay exactly where he was in Redmond, Oregon. Despite offers of moving out of state to more attractive circumstances (house and real property), he did not want to relocate anywhere else. Notwithstanding vigorous arm twisting, he emphatically told me (and in no uncertain terms) that he wanted to be in geographical proximity to his children. No matter how big the carrot was dangled in front of his nose, James told me in his usual pleasant and gentlemanly manner that, "My kids are the most important thing on my mind and in my life."

PARANOIA

While in Alaska, a German (sprechen sie Deutsch) security-bodyguard appeared on the Gold Rush scene. Unbeknownst to any of us, some speculated it may have been connected to the 2010 hostage incident at Discovery's headquarters in Washington D.C. where the lone gunman of Asian descent was killed by police.

I planted a seed of doubt or mystery when I interviewed this security guy about his background. He said that he didn't work for an organization or company but solo. Somewhere along the line, the subject of kidnapping came up – it was an integral part of any security matters. His face turned pale as he tried to compose himself after I asked if he had any experience in hostage negotiations.

After a few seconds, he said, "I'll find someone (in this field) that can handle negotiations."

At that point the bodyguard/security man became a little more reclusive or drawn in.

More than a few days later, he lowered or dropped his guard to become more socially welcomed and accepted. He smiled as he came into Dave's RV wearing a hardhat (which didn't fit properly) and accepted a couple bottles of delicious smoked salmon that I shared with everyone. It was not long thereafter our German friend left. Whether he later reported our conversation or not, I'm sure RAW reported the home invasion incident that was thwarted by Kato in Jack's RV at the Gold Rush RV campground in Dawson City.

I cannot nor will I speculate any ties to this or my "welcome" that RAW and Discovery gave me on the day I went to see Todd at the mine site (regarding matters of obtaining our own television channel). I was held up for several minutes from reaching it and I didn't know the reason(s) for this – whether they were filming or if something else happened. Eventually, clearance was given and I was escorted to the frontage of the mine site and then was ceremoniously blocked from entering. I didn't understand why I was banned since I had been there before to deliver supplies and equipment. Moreover, as I was driving along this same road an hour earlier, I bumped into a couple in their vehicle who said, "Just left visiting the mine site with the Gold Rush cast."

As I chatted with RAW supervisors (and thereby stalling me for several more minutes), an SUV came down from the road with occupants who introduced themselves from the Discovery Channel. They offered me the opportunity to accompany them back to Dawson City – this was after my 60 hour drive from California - can you believe that? I politely thanked them and waited until I finished my mission to meet with Todd.

Paranoia, apprehension, selective bias - you judge for yourself. I think it could have been a simple case of misunderstanding on their part. My reluctance in providing every dot and tittle of personal information must have raised a red flag in their own eyes, especially in light of that unfortunate incident that occurred relatively recently at their headquarters. Or, word from an earlier discussion (that touched upon the subject of kidnapping) with the German security person could have been the cause of suspicion.

At any rate, there was more mounting pressure by Discovery to secure more releases and identity checks for Kato. Todd, his crew and Kato brushed them aside. At least that was the appearance that I got.

GENERAL TODD

Todd's role as "General" required him to command a torrent of emotional levels and nuances of different personalities on his team. Todd is not intimidating and yet at the same time pathetic. Off camera, he tears your heart out (gently at first and then later with more rigor). This mix of interaction is interesting to watch. Todd is a person who has within him the seeds of greatness; he could never sprout the seeds while being inundated with distractions that could have been assumed by those delegated with that authority to address them (please refer to the memo I wrote to him on page 39).

Everyone, and I mean everyone - Discovery Channel executives in Alaska, the Yukon, Los Angeles and Washington D.C. HQ, as well as on-site crewmen, had difficulty at times in working with Todd. Negotiations were frequently interrupted by ad hoc "strikes". If he didn't like what was going on, Todd would pull off the body microphones, pull his cast members off the shoot and announce another work stoppage. In situations where salary payments were not met in a timely fashion for example, Todd quits until resolution was made to his liking. Union reps may want to hire Todd as an effective consultant.

Many in the hallways of Discovery HQ found Todd to be one of the most difficult to work with. He's very disciplined, when he chooses to be. He spends a lot of time getting to know cast and crew alike and how we cope with the "why me" periods of our lives. If there is moral to Todd's Gold Rush, it is that he leaves himself open and available to the surprising contradictions in life and at the end he finds strength to go on.

Todd's demeanor of conducting business subtly or overtly is pretty much the same - it's "do it my way or it's the highway". Men who are drafted in service should always be treated fairly and equitably despite drawbacks that situations always present. Whenever possible, bring the deposed party privately out of the limelight and see if you can iron out any flaws or shortcomings from both sides. Otherwise, leadership will take its toll when you end up in the front with no one following you but your shadow.

METAMORPHOSIS

Intrepid or timid? I say neither, but somewhere nearer the former. That is how one may perceive Todd's conception of Gold Rush, which took place more than seven years ago. Sure, he worked in the corporate world, achieved entrepreneurial success and realized financial gain on different levels and fronts; one may find this to be an adequate foundation to build upon.

Todd always emphatically tells me he knows TV. Whether that may have been the idea of captivating an audience every week or generating inordinate amounts of money by making sponsors pay a television station to pay you, it seems that someone has lost his original dream. To me, and more importantly as many would agree, is the question of "What is the price in achieving that success?" Lost personal convictions and the trail of bodies left behind were the costs of assembling Gold Rush.

It's very easy to go Monday morning quarterbacking when you don't have to walk in Todd's shoes. When everyone is criticizing you on the basis of salaries, equipment and fuel expenditures, food, film footage, remarks made on the show, portrayals that were made up and torn down – the entire gamut of producing a television show seems overwhelming, to say nothing of the least. Todd had to wear so many hats that his head seemed gargantuan. Besides being the General in the military sense, Todd had to wear the hats of logistics, signal corp, chaplain corp, and so on. He had no real staff officers to consult with or to fall back on except with the nightly use of the internet. Kato pointed out to Todd that there was a great need to delegate some responsibility in order for him to focus on the core issues. Each night, written proposals and parole evidence were made by Kato to remind Todd of his need to have more down time for himself – mentally, physically and spiritually - as well as time for planning and strategy. At times you need to step back, return later and see things from a totally different perspective. Implementation will definitely be on an easier path. These proposals were "read" but filed in deep six (proverbially. I retrieved them from incineration.

Instead of a well-oiled machine, chaos was the result. Hey, maybe that's what Todd wanted people to see - chaos. Maybe that's what makes the audience glued to their seats for an hour on Friday evenings. Who wants to see a precision military battalion march in perfect unison under Garryowen week after week? (except those few and proud). If that is the case, then plan on having a well-ordered sequence of chaotic episodes without risking life or limb or at least the bare minimum, the personal health and well-being of your men. Remember, it is the leader's utmost responsibility for the accomplishment of the mission without undue risk in maintaining the welfare of your men (both physically and mentally). You cannot compromise one without directly affecting the other. I don't have to tell you that your men will always follow you in loyalty so long they are treated accordingly. You can look throughout our military history (battles fought and won) and see the correlation between the victories and the courage that loyalty endears from leaders.

BAD TASTE IN THEIR MOUTH

It became clear that both RAW and Discovery had no love loss for me. First, since there was no legal consideration on my behalf, there should likewise be no legal requirement or duty to fulfill on my behalf. Simple. Waivers and nondisclosures required of me were not held tenable. I was the guest of the Hoffmans.

Second, I appeared to preoccupy Todd with my advisory roles. Discovery took that preoccupation as a distraction. I agree. To reiterate. I serve at the pleasure of the Hoffmans, not Discovery. Like every president that occupies the Oval Office, he requires an undated letter of resignation from everyone. From the Cabinet down to each appointee, they all serve at the pleasure of the president. When he no longer needs that individual or finds that individual unsuitable because of deviating policy that was once commonly shared, the president pulls out that letter from the bottom left-hand, locked drawer and has it processed for his/her dismissal as their resignation.

Considerable effort was made for me to cooperate in signing papers that have no legal, equitable basis. I was told throughout my stay by members of the cast, Todd's crew, as well as by RAW, that I needed to find a niche in the storyline to explain my appearance in front of the camera. As mentioned previously, I did not take it seriously by pulling out my signature line of, "peeling potatoes at the Sandy McDonald's when Jack found me."

As a result, my "uninvited" appearance on some of the episodes shot with or without my knowledge had to be erased or removed from the actual broadcasts, an expense in both time and cost. I wasn't awestruck or anything with television celebrities, especially after previously meeting the Jimmy Stewarts, Ronald Reagans and the Charlton Hestons of the silver screen or the Jay Lenos and Tom Sellecks of television. Therefore, I made considerable effort to avoid the camera wherever they shot by going the long way around them. In fact, when I was helping James (at his request) by using a drill to sand down the jagged edges of some metal piping, I kept turning my posterior in the direction in which they were trying to shoot.

It was never my intent to be a thorn in their side and I apologize for being a bad taste in their mouth.

HOLLYWOOD

After Chris spoke to me regarding the methodology of speaking in front of a camera (where I always exclaimed, "You gotta be kidding me"), James told me the following:

"Go for it. You might become the next TV idol"; we both laughed.
"Be candid when you're doing work and try not to go Hollywood."
I said, "What's Hollywood?"
"Going Hollywood is working on the mine project only when the cameras are rolling."
I said, "I see. But what about doing things that RAW asks of you, like re-shooting if they forgot to reinsert a new memory card to record footage?"
"Ignore it. Do your job and everything else will fall into place. Shoot from the hip and tell it like it is."
I said, "I'll just do my job, even fetching cool clear water for the guys. If I get into the shot, too bad. I don't care if I accidentally walk in on a long distance shot. My mission is to help the guys physically."
"Go for it, partner."

During the flag raising ceremony at Porcupine Creek, Todd pulled me over to instruct them (Jim) in the proper way of raising a flag.

I said to Jim, "This is the way. First, don't dare let the American flag touch the ground. Unless you have another (American) flag available, I'm required to burn it if you do. Spread out the flag, connect it to the rope pulley and pull the flag up quickly without stopping."

I returned to my position out of the camera shoot (so I thought) and Jim connected the flag to the rope pulley. Instead of raising the flag quickly to the top of the flagpole, Jim jerked it up in stages, pausing in between intervals.

Having served in color guard I said to myself, "everyone is going to see this being done in a disrespectful way."

Tim Dalby, who was one of RAW's great professionals at the top of his game and most appreciated by Todd's crew (always spoken highly of in every breath), came over to me to explain that, "We meant no disrespect."

I replied, "Many men's blood were spilled for that flag."

After I composed myself, I saw a camera lens reflecting in the sunlight apparently filming from a distance, perched from an elevated position. I thought nothing of it until later when Todd became more insistent of having me in front of the camera. We talked more about the gravity of the mission this show would have and the greater ramifications it would have on the whole picture. Todd intimated that I shouldn't think of myself on an individual basis but rather as one sacrificing himself for the good and better of the whole. You sometimes don't have a leg to stand on when arguing with Todd. In fact, I couldn't agree with him more. His logic is often incontrovertible. However, I still have to live with myself knowing this episodic venture will end sooner or later and then it'll be weighed out to see if it was worth it all.

In the end, I took the high road. As I usually say, "When in doubt, get out."

Later at the Sandy Airport, Todd presented me a folded flag (in an encased box) - one that was flown over the U.S. Capitol. He knew how I felt about Old Glory. My mouth dropped. For the first time, I gave Todd a hug. Like Mike Fox, I wasn't a tree hugger.

A majority of the Gold Rush cast says that Todd has gone Hollywood. Staging became more important and using it in atypical, unprofessional fashion became more predominant as the mining season went along. It became noticeable that Todd, Jack and Jim spent more time inside their own RVs than actually doing physical mining work – this according to James' observation. Dave, Greg and Chris had strenuous, monotonous work that lasted many hours longer. Monday morning quarterbacking is easy when you consider Jack was suffering an increasingly debilitative back problem (an operation would be needed), Todd was addressing daily planning and strategy, and Jim finding new replacements for his mustaches (self-deprecation?).

Before filming the new season of Gold Rush, Greg departed weeks earlier than the others in order to prep the mining site by removing the slush or permafrost layers of the ground so that it would make it easier for excavation. As the mining season got into the third and fourth quarters, Todd, Jack and Jim were accused of coming out of their RVs only when filming required them to appear. After the shoot was over, "Todd, Jack and Jim usually returned back to their sanctuaries of comfort", according to another Gold Rush cast member.

In addition, James said he felt some members of the group came out of their RVs for certain shots demanded in filming (frequently dictated by cast members) and then immediately returned when shooting concluded. This was done irrespective of finishing the actual mining work that needed to be done. Some guys chose to put themselves first rather than doing more physically demanding mining work.

Pacing themselves also stretched out the number of weekly episodes, thus equating to fatter paychecks. If there is nothing to shoot except for mundane labor, then something had to be created for dramatic footage. Without the ability to look inside other people's heads, we may speculate that their priority shifted from team work to personal attention of oneself. This would have spawned, perhaps, into friction between cast members. Their priority of honest team work may have shifted to looking out for number one.

Some may even have paced themselves by not giving 100% of themselves all the time; this was very critical in situations where one aspect of work was dependent upon another. For example, in the second season in the Yukon, it was fatefully learned that the removal of permafrost needed to be done earlier in the mining season before the warmer summer climate turned it into plain, unworkable and dangerous slush (Wayne Fisher pointed this out to me very early on since it was common knowledge to any simpleton who mines up in the Yukon). Incidents of both Greg and Dave dangerously slipping and sliding in their dozers made for some serious film footage. As a result of this, Greg was sent up to the Yukon several weeks ahead to perform this boring but necessary task (unspectacular to television audience, but a routine commanding extreme risk and danger) without much fanfare and filming. Greg took his mark and did his job like a real man – he did it without recognition.

As a further testament to scripted drama, this corollary proves that Todd already knew and preemptively made up his mind as to where mining would take place for the new mining season. In other words, there was no need to find the gold, just dig it up. To reiterate, confirming the location of gold generally consumes 99.999% of typical gold mining. We'll discuss this later.

Sidebar. Whenever they stopped working, RAW stopped shooting and resumed the next day where they left off. RAW had one of their crew members write down the exact clothing description of each cast member before the camera lens were turned off so that they would dress the same to finish the shoot "uninterrupted" the next day. This was a practice once reserved for shooting theatrical movies and broadcast television comedies and dramas, not "reality" TV.

REALITY TV?

How to put Kato in front of the camera. Todd couldn't figure out a plausible storyline that explained how he procured funding for this latest mining venture. This was especially needful after he made a proclamation for financial help on the first season's last episode. A few days later, Todd asked me to become "The Investor". He racked his brain and even asked Chris to "teach" me the lexicon of communicating in front of a camera. I've been on more than one national television network and furthermore, for fun, played a role as an extra in Clint Eastwood's last Dirty Harry movie saga. I've even offered my views with the 41st President on which son should make a run for the White House.

I just said to Todd,   "It ain't gonna be real."
Todd replied,   "It doesn't matter."

I said, "Isn't this supposed to be reality TV?"
Todd just smiled and winked.

Moreover, I still didn't want to sign anything more than what I'd already signed for RAW and Discovery. They still kept after me wanting more disclosure and releases. If they didn't like it, I gave my usual line: "I serve at the pleasure of the Hoffmans." It was believed that I could have been in too many scenes shot for them to remove if I declined permission to do so. I didn't care if they shot me or not. Besides, there were some scenes in which Kato was shown on Gold Rush and nobody filed any estoppel action for that. Todd was pressured and eventually gave in to Discovery.

Bottom line, when Todd has to scrape the bottom of the barrel in using Kato for the show, it just shows you how desperate and low a man can go.

WHY GO WITH GOLD RUSH?

Up until that time, I had traveled to forty countries and 49 states. I think you already know which state I hadn't been to yet. So when the subject of Alaska came up, I told Jack that I had never traveled with a tour group in my life, nor would I complete the visit of every state by going on an Alaskan cruise. I don't like crowds and I prefer the wide open spaces. Except for normal business and foreign trade missions organized by government officials, I'm a lone wolf that likes the adventure of traveling without hotel reservations or preset agendas from the likes of Lonely Planet (travel guides and agents). Bearing in mind, I haven't subscribed to cable television since the end of Gold Rush season one. So rather than extend my cable subscription for another year to watch Gold Rush, why not accompany them (per Jack and Todd's invitation and request)? I of course was offered the opportunity to accompany the production team of BATTLEGROUND to Europe but I had just finished a trip that consisted of spending a month in each of the six continents within a period of six months, which already included Europe. It would have been seven continents in seven months but a major earthquake in the southern tip of Argentina precluded my plans to visit Antarctica. I'll do the 7/7 after my next trip to …. (already planned).

As discussed previously and far from their (everyone's) knowledge, I didn't want to watch Gold Rush as it was being produced for television as a spectator but rather as a contributor immersed in their welfare. I had already participated in the production of feature films, observed movies being produced in California, Hong Kong and Europe, stood in the back stages of Broadway, sat more than once in the audience of every late network

TV show in New York (Letterman & others) and Los Angeles (Leno & O'Brien in San Francisco for a week). I didn't want to watch Gold Rush from a sofa at home nor just be on their set watching it as it was being filmed. I, too, thought of this trip as my mission to help Todd and his crew to accomplish their mission.

Having said that, by watching and learning to not repeat mistakes seen in season one, I asked and received assistance from James to make sure that all of our vehicles were serviced and maintained. This included James' procurement and servicing of Jim's new 3500 GMC dually. We purchased tools primarily from Harbor Freight so that James wouldn't need to sacrifice losing his Snap On and other custom tools as he did in season one. Finally, we purchased gas and diesel fuel, fluids and spare parts for the trucks, first aid and hygienic supplies, medicine, vitamins and other supplements, solar-powered lanterns, lights, and showers, nutritional foods and drinks, walkie-talkies - you get the picture that I am proactive and not passive.

Bottom line: I did not want to be a liability on this or any other mission.

ROMNEY & GOLD

Before Greg and Chris returned back to Sandy and after we looked at some possible television programming that I wanted to produce, we had an opportunity to appear at a rally for Republican Presidential candidate Mitt Romney. I turned down the offer from them since they wanted these Gold Rush TV stars to endorse Romney indirectly and not on the same stage. They would have served much like a greeter or a doorman at the Waldorf Astoria.

Once I returned them to Oregon, I told them that I needed unique gifts as door openers for several more major investors for the new TV channel that was planned. They provided gold from the second season as well as documented photos .

Greg carefully weighed his one ounce gold out for me and his very great son whispers to his father, "Give him (Kato) a discount." To wit, Greg charged me $1,300 (prevailing price of PURE, refined gold was around $1,300). At Chris' home, he weighed out his gold, had his photo taken and gave them outright to me as a gift.

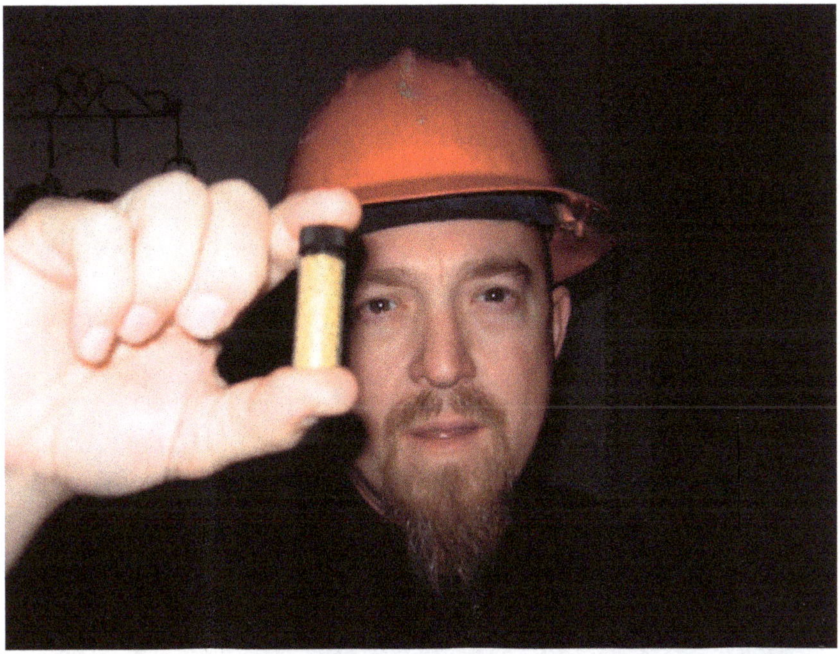

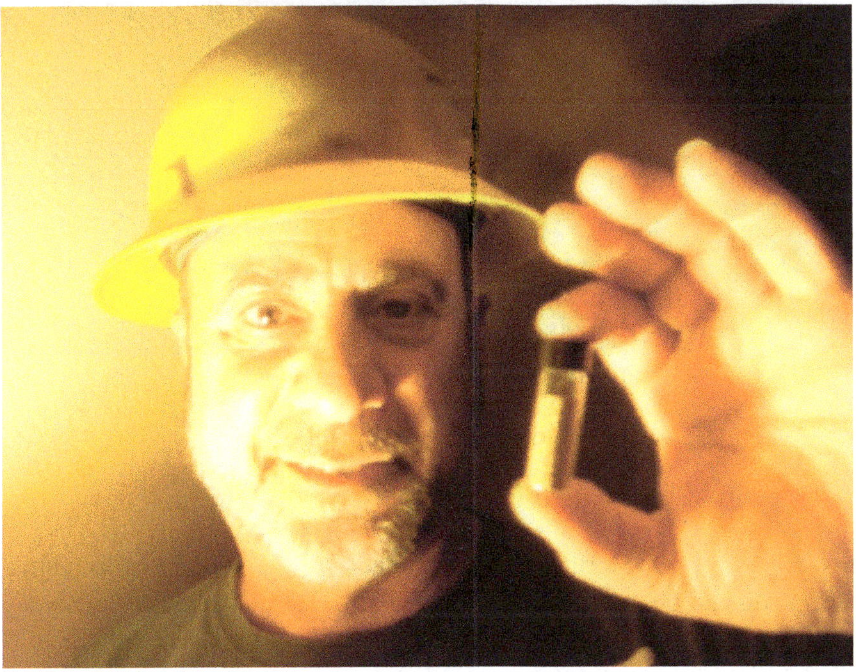

At the Silver Dollar Queen in Virginia City

A SLIP OF A LIP

    Active military and veterans know the adage of "A slip of a lip can sink a ship." No greater scripting can be made in Gold Rush than this.
    When Dan Russell and I had our weekly or biweekly phone conversations, he mentioned that Mike Fox was very depressed and on the verge of something possibly worse. This was after Mike refused to accept an offer to work security for Todd at the Yukon site that was at a pay scale half the normal rate, this according to Dan. As a result,

Todd asked Mike to leave the Sandy Airport where he was residing. I needed to get in touch with Todd but, again, the phone number changed, so I called Jim Thurber instead.

I called Jim to relay an important message about Mike Fox (at the end of the third season) and Jim says, "How are you doing....Can you help me Kato in getting a new RV trailer home?"

Looking into a mirror, I said to myself: "Do I look like an ATM now?"

I said to him, "Jim, why and how are you going to bring it down there? Aren't you guys heading for Sudamerica for season four?"

Jim says, "Yeah, I'll be gone for just a year."

I said, "Wait, what do you mean?"

Jim says, "The new RV is not for there but for the Yukon."

I said, "Wait a minute. You want to use the new RV in the Yukon next year (season 5) and be in South America for just one season, and not for several good or bad mining seasons?"

In his next breath I hear on the phone, a long silent pause.

I said to myself,

"Why, since they are leaving for Guyana? He said he needs it for the Yukon for the fifth season."

Therefore, Jim, as well as Todd, Jack and Dave, and Discovery of course, all knew ahead of time that the South American venture was a one shot deal and not to be extended beyond a year, barring the find of the legendary lost Aztec treasure. After a long pause to "let this 'leak' sink in", I concluded our phone conversation by saying that I wasn't able to assist him in securing a new RV for the Yukon under the present circumstances I was in. After more friendly exchanges with Jim, I gave my usual inquiry of :

"When are you gonna take me elk hunting?"

Jim is an experienced outdoor sportsman and professional guide and told me that he once worked with John Wayne in that capacity. Talk about name droppers! My mouth dropped. He's one of my heroes and I have nothing less than a nice collection of the Duke's memorabilia. I've visited the John Wayne birthplace home in Winterset, Iowa a couple of times, which is not too far from Ronald Reagan's birthplace in Tampico, Illinois. They are great, inspirational places to visit. I highly recommend both of these as vacation destinations.

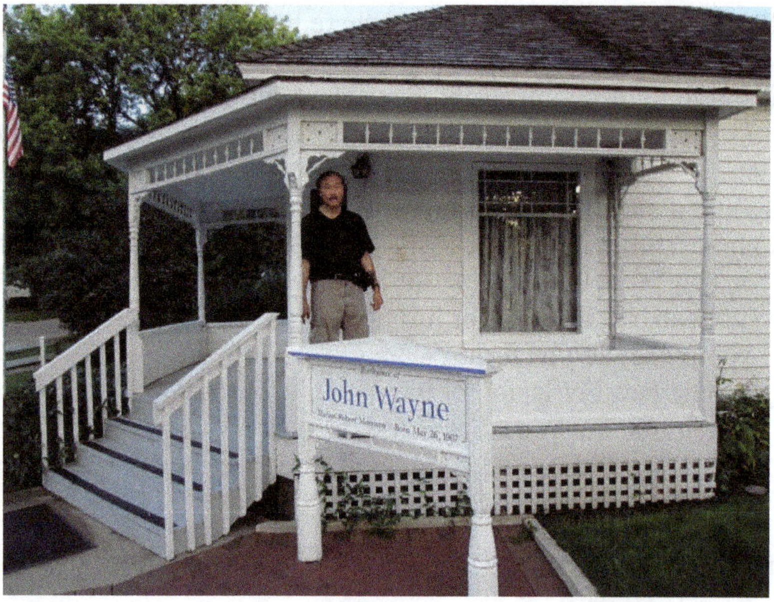
John Wayne

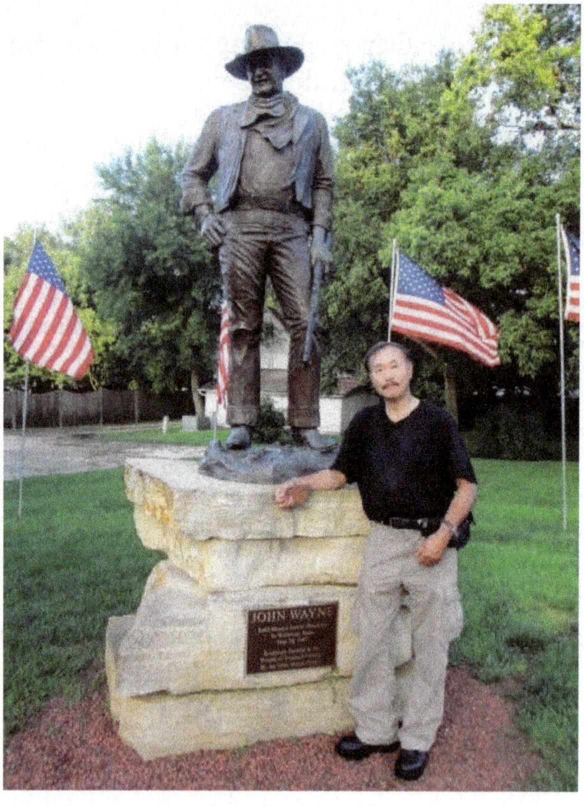
JOHN WAYNE

With pretty much that, we concluded our pleasant conversation and I told him to be cool. I never thought much about the significance of Jim's statement until I ran into some Gold Rush aficionados at a restaurant. They told me that Todd said that he is pulling stakes out of Guyana and was returning to gold mining in the Yukon.

I said to them, "Wasn't it just a venture to last for just one year?" They gave me one resounding "NO".

One individual said that there must have been considerable capital outlays for transportation, heavy equipment, fuel, supplies, and even the construction of their permanent housing (even though volunteers came all the way from Todd's own church to build it).

Therefore, a one shot single season for South America was planned all along. Jim knew that South America was a one season diversion that would allow Todd to restart another three-year cycle. That would rekindle interest and follows the format of the beginning of a new recycled serial (season five) - refer to page 24.

LEAVING GOLD RUSH

Why did Todd ask Kato to leave Gold Rush? At first, he said, "To look for investors for our new TV channel." That's true and it brought me back later to the Yukon as well as to Sandy, Oregon. Notwithstanding the ongoing pressure from Discovery to remove my presence from the mining site, the Hoffmans and the crew stood fast behind me (as far as I can tell).

I noticed one day that while everyone was working on rehabilitating Wayne's shaker/wash plant, Chris was grabbing one side of his face, grimacing in pain. After learning this reason for his loud snoring and Jim's late night returns to their shared RV, it was time to secure Chris a place of his own. With no afterthought, Chris returned the favor by offering to replicate his carpentry skills in Porcupine Creek and construct a cabin for me at the Yukon mining site. My thinking would be to share the cabin and relinquish "title" back to Todd or any other team member when I left. For whatever reason, Todd did not want a permanent structure on that property where mining was taking place. That was my impression with the intimations that Todd made. Whatever excuse it was that prompted him to ask for my departure, Todd asked me to immediately tap my source(s) to fund our new cable TV channel.

After checking with law firms and banks that specialized in media acquisitions, it was learned that acquiring a new cable channel didn't pose any material or FCC problems. The real issue was finding enough content to fill the new station's weekly 168 hour quota. That to me was the challenge Todd and I needed more personal, face to face consultation.

EVICTIONS

The following were told to me from either the victim or the evictor. Mike Fox, one of the original "Three Musketeers", provided professional business support to Todd. When Todd rejected Mike for not accompanying him to the Yukon as security-bodyguard for the third season (because of a salary dispute) he either quit or was released and asked to leave the Sandy Airport where he lived with his great and talented son, Talon. Mike demanded and received back pay and compensation - this included pay for products and merchandise brought in through placements shown on Gold Rush and delivered to the Sandy Airport (firearms, Arctic Cat ATVs, cold weather gear, camping products, significant equipment and personal and commercial endorsements.)

There seems to be a history. When James quit the show, Todd asked him to leave the airport. Without a doubt, James had the most things to move out of the airport when he was asked to leave. The equipment alone was tantamount to moving an artillery battalion when his dilapidated physical condition was put into consideration. Auto and truck hoists had to be unbolted from the concrete, heavy equipment and tools packed and re-loaded, trucks, motorcycles and autos moved, including a showroom car once offered to and considered by Jay Leno, musical instruments and drum sets dismantled - all to be readied and relocated hundreds of miles away.

Greg was asked to leave the Yukon during the second season because of alcoholism. He was asked to return later under the guise of failing to gain willful employment back in Oregon. Greg finished the second season with Todd in the Yukon.

Chris' interrogation by Todd and his group in the third season must have been the straw that broke the camel's back. He had enough and decided to quit the show altogether.

At the conclusion of the third season, the host of an After Show declared that a major announcement(s) from key members of the cast was about to take place, right after commercial interruption of course. With all eyes peeled on Todd, the announcer and camera panned over to Chris and he says he is not returning and wants to move on. Greg, sitting next to Chris, announces his intention to quit mining. I don't know whether or not anyone knew beforehand of these resignations but it did serve its purpose in adding drama and ratings. With respect to Parker, he announces his intention to pull up stakes from Alaska and go mining in the Yukon; he makes a passionate plea for help up there. Turning his head and looking in the direction of Greg and Chris, Parker solicits help from the two. Greg needs work. Greg acquiesces almost immediately and Chris thinks about it.

Later in the year, Chris relents and chooses to work with Parker. Before making a public decision during the next mining season, Chris was asked to bring some heavy equipment up to the Yukon on his truck. I'm not sure whether Chris wanted to go back to mining or not but after the delivery was made for his friend, he set about to rejoin with Greg and work on Parker's team.

Remembering Parker's solicitation of Chris to join his team, Chris said to me, "it wasn't about money" but rather a mentorship with Parker that could ameliorate his relationship with Discovery and others around him. Chris had always been a great "people" person and well known for his charity of helping others (carpentry, money, mentoring, time). [During the first Gold Rush season, Chris built a cabin for Greg's family in Porcupine Creek]. Parker's abusive language was well known and deservedly censored by RAW/Discovery. It was believed to be a win-win situation for everyone except Todd. Chris was invaluable as a worker; he was loyal and committed to the accomplishment of the mission.

Today, although Greg lives across the street and down a little ways from Todd's airport home, decades of friendly buddy conversation between the two have now given way to just friendly hand gestures and occasional sparse words - this according to Greg.

AFTER GOLD RUSH

Needless to say, I haven't checked my imaginary crystal ball to see what these men intend to do with their lives after they are no longer involved with filming the Gold Rush series. Based upon my discussions with them, I am going to take a stab or two at what may transpire for them.

Todd: As he told me, Todd wants to permeate Hollywood with positive and uplifting television shows. Having introduced an entirely new genre which has been copied and replicated by Discovery and other television channels, he would have virtually no problem in getting attention to develop another new series (if he hasn't already). Moreover, with syndication revenue soon backing him up, he may be able to produce shows totally independent of editing issues that he had been facing. Nevertheless, even if Todd took an abbreviated respite of a year or so, he can at least say, "been there, done that". I have the utmost confidence that the next show he creates and produces will be even more exciting and command a wider audience.

Jack: What can you say to a man who has successfully achieved almost everything he has chosen to pursue? Just look around him and you can truly see the definition of what a man for all seasons really is. Beyond the secular sense, there is nothing greater in the world than having a family that everyone admires. Knowing his selflessness from the time he served his country in the Army to currently helping Todd, Jack will continue to put his family, friends and others first and himself last.

Greg: As a man with excellent business acumen, I see Greg continuing to find more corporate relationships as a company spokesman and endorser of various products. More importantly, it is hoped that Greg will not lose his strong desire to serve God by sharing his testimony through speaking engagements in churches and other organizations (as he has been doing).

Jim: Without the harsh reality of monetary demands, it is believed that Jim may return to his first love in some capacity as a professional outdoorsman. He will be able to choose among very select clients in the entertainment and corporate world, as he did before. I was told by Chris that Jim (though he lives in Portland and not in Sandy) comes to the Sandy Airport frequently to help in doing whatever work was needed. Jim told me that he intended to open a soup kitchen-charity somewhere nearby.

Chris: Chris tells me that he wants to make one of my program treatments a reality show called "Wounded Warriors", namesake of the wonderful organization helping our military servicemen to retrench themselves back into civilian life. After hiring a private single-engine prop to take Jack, Chris and myself to Merrill Field in Anchorage, Alaska to meet with guests, sponsors and representatives of Wounded Warriors, we were absolutely impressed with this very fine organization and the work that they proudly perform. Chris wants to MC each week by hosting one individual with his or her story of reaching their particular point of time. He wants to entertain them with an outdoor event - hunting, fishing, mountain climbing, trekking or whatever adventure they choose. Each episode would show the challenges and triumphs of individual humanity. During seasonal breaks, Chris would likely need to take time off and relax with his family and speak at various venues without monetary compensation. He desires to focus on inner-city youth.

Dave: Although I do not specifically know what pursuits Dave will have once the cameras stop rolling on Gold Rush, multitalented and multidimensional Dave will have no trouble in pursuing whatever endeavor He chooses for him. Dave clearly understands that he'll be happiest knowing that he is in God's will.

Kato: Having met queens, prime ministers, statesmen (including every President since Nixon, except one) and citizens of more than 40 countries around the world, I have had no greater privilege than working with the most exceptional men anyone can ever meet. It is hoped that these friendships of Gold Rush will continue.

Though my years of travel that have taken me from the jungles of Southeast Asia and the Amazon to the deserts of Africa and the Australian Outback, wait and see what happens this summer as preparations are underway for what promises to be the most exciting adventure I have ever taken.

MUNDANE LIVING

Anyone who reports to duty or stamps in his time card will tell you how difficult it can be at times when one faces daily tasks consisting of hard physical, laborious work. It takes a certain level of mental drive to keep it going, especially with a two or three-person camera crew following and recording every move and sound you make. After the day's mining work is done, you retire to your trailer, look yourself in the mirror and ask yourself:

"Is this worth it?" or "What in the world am I doing here?" "I can be at home right now with my family and taking it easy. I don't need this!"

It takes a lot of introspection every day and night. As the old saying goes, "You just have to play the cards you have been dealt with."

Recognizing the fact that the greater the complexity of work, the greater the need for the simplicity of play. There is virtually no form of diversion or recreation in that remote and isolated part of the world. Except for what each man brought up with him in his RV, rarely does Todd, Jack, Jim, Greg, Dave, Chris or James interact socially or even have simple quiet time for themselves. With the intervention of a spouse and/or kids visiting, it would be only for a few weeks or so.

Like every household, when you come home from work you want to get out of your work clothes, wash and clean up. (There is limited RV water so we go into town and find and then pay for a quick shower. While Jim was taking a shower at the Gold Rush RV campground, his clothes were being washed/dried at a self-service laundromat. A souvenir collector ran off with his large canvas bag that carried his wash. It seems star power has its liabilities even in the Yukon. Postscript: For me, it's not worth chasing after, although I could have since I was sitting there waiting for my turn to shower. (Plastered on restaurant walls in Dawson City were photos of the previous luminaries who just recently completed filming in town-Steve Martin, Jack Black and Owen Wilson.) After preparing dinner (macaroni or boil a pack or two of Ramen noodles – Jack's usual or getting some "fast food" (no Carl's Jr./Wendy's/McDonald's per regulatory edict in historically preserved Dawson City, relax a bit by watching your favorite baseball team and/or NBA finals in June and take a short nap (usually long). Unfortunately, these guys can't do that up there. Restaurants are expensive (e.g. CDN. $18, U.S. $21 hamburgers) and everything is practically closed for the evening by the time they get into town. With Parker's team operating in an even more remote location than Todd's group, Greg and Chris now work six days a week and for longer hours. Since the fourth Gold Rush season, they are more geographically isolated and are now facing a much greater physical and mental challenge under Parker.

In any event, it still takes a certain amount of strength drawn from a higher source to see you through each day. When the last episode from the last season is over, you can believe that the sacrifice of family separation, daily physical pain and deprivation of simple conveniences and personal privacy will have Greg, Chris Dave, Jim, Jack and Todd looking in the mirror and whispering to themselves, "It was worth it all!"

IDIOSYNCRASIES

"I'm Late, I'm Late, I'm Late"

[White Rabbit sayings by Charles Lutwidge Dodgson (pseudonym Lewis Carroll)]

In any convoys, all drivers stop in unison whenever a member vehicle encounters mechanical difficulties or for whatever reason that requires stoppage. Obviously, the lead vehicle commands inerrantly, i.e., Todd's will. In the case of trucks that follow Todd, Greg (for example) needed a pit stop so he pulled over. Meanwhile Todd tells him on the walkie-talkie to hurry and catch up with the rest of them as he and the convoy continues rolling! James, taking on the role of emergency repair vehicle and dogging the herd (as you cowboys would say), wryly smiles and lingers back waiting for Greg (and son). It was a good thing that he did so because we saw Greg make the wrong turn; we redirected him back to the convoy.

****

Remembering Clothes

After shooting ends for the day, a member of RAW makes a recording on a clipboard: everybody's clothes are noted so that they can resume filming where they left off. One of the RAW guys that we invited with us to eat at Diamond Tooth Gertie's, a very large and historic turn of the century gambling hall with live stage show performances, commented to me that they never needed to know what I would wear the next day since I always wear a black tee-shirt, a black wind breaker, khaki pants and black shoes (I brought a case of black tees and khaki's from Walmart in the lower 48). It's the same attire I have been wearing for the last twenty or so years - I don't have very much imagination. The point is, is this reality TV?)

****

When GoPro Goes Off

During our drive up to Alaska and after RAW's GoPro camera turned itself off (outside the truck's front windshield), James said that during the first season at Porcupine Creek, he guarded the camp while Todd and the others went to Haines for food and fun. Feeling left out, James said that he was going to take it easier this time around by not overexerting himself to the point of physical collapse (because of his back condition). Not yet knowing what he was going to do, James did not fully reveal to me the severity of his true condition until he left the show and when accompanied him to hospitals and medical specialists.

****

2 Heads Are Better Than 1

Todd told me that he intended to use two different types of wash plants in the next (third) season: the same that he was already using and a new, cylinder-rolling version. Todd soon realized that splitting his team backfired in more ways than he ever expected. James told me, "Todd must have seen the handwriting on the wall when he tried to split his team into two. He must have known that he was losing control of the show and needed something new or spectacular to reign in the audience." By losing control, it meant that RAW was shooting two other competing teams, Dakota Fred and Parker - with or without Todd's knowledge at this particular point of time.

****

Real Alaskan Gold

While in Alaska, certain people went to a post office to retrieve their mail, which (I was told) included royalty checks from Alaskan State oil revenue. The royalty checks from oil subsidies in the State of Alaska were entitled to every Alaskan citizen for oil revenue produced annually. These checks amounted to thousands of dollars. Invitation was offered for me to become eligible in receiving these royalty checks but I declined, since I was just passing through.

****

Homes

In terms of homes that I have been invited to, Chris' forte was clearly evident in his beautifully designed custom home. If he ever needed to quit his "day-time job", Chris can revert back to his first career as a carpenter. He should not have any difficulty in other roles such as a high-demand consultant in several professional areas: television production and directing, logistics, speaking engagements, community relations and so forth. In recognizing his talent, I wanted Chris to serve as lead designer for a new show that I have in mind. However, as previously mentioned, Chris wishes to choose "Wounded Warriors" as his first television assignment to head.

The first time that I visited James' home in Redmond, he gave me a tour of his new spread that included several acres. When we returned to the main house, James showed me photos before it had been remodeled. I couldn't believe what I saw and told him to stop pulling my leg - he told me that it was initially comprised of two portable trailer homes. In order to allay the high cost of leasehold rent, James did both the plumbing and rewiring as well as other areas of reconstruction and improvements; this was further testament to his talent and ability.

Greg's brand new beautiful home sits further back behind his original small frontage property along the road. It was last (2014) Christmas weekend morning that I entered his unlocked gated property to drop off some treats, which I hung onto his doorknob. I didn't want to disturb Greg and his family that early in the morning. I wanted to drop the same confectioneries to Jack and Todd's home but I forgot the code numbers to gain passage through the gate. Upon returning to Chris' home and seeing that the initial boxes of cookies were gone, I had doubts of whether I was even at the right house to begin with. Before leaving more cookies on the doorknob, I investigated the truck parked adjacent to this house - a blue F350 with work gloves inside the cab. As I was verbalizing to myself, "This gotta be the right place", Chris wildly swings open the door, causing me to belch out my surprise – there are very few times in which I had ever been caught off guard like I had at that moment.

****

Wayne's Motive

Wayne Fishers' motive (as he told me) in helping Todd's team, RAW and the Gold Rush production was "To gain respect from his brother, not just making more money." In other words, Wayne wanted to be one up on his brother.

****

3:16

The idea of having tee-shirts and other merchandise/items printed with 3:16 was suggested by Kato when he saw Todd autographing photos by just signing his name. I suggested that Todd should complement Jack's "No Guts, No Glory" phrase with the inscription of "John 3:16". Todd liked this idea so I promoted it by giving it to everyone (including my friends and VIPs with his autograph and this inscription on Gold Rush promotional photo handouts.

****

Freaking, whatever

This is a word construed by many as an expletive in lieu of an out-and-out curse word. Todd started to use it in the show and it became more frequently used as an adjective. I have not personally heard Todd use that word in conversation with me. Apparently this kind of vocabulary sits well within the show and not in his personal life. I was dismayed when I heard it being used by Todd's own boys in Sandy after the season's completion.

****

Beer & Jokes

Whenever key words like those mentioned in the foregoing are used by Todd, crowds in bars, clubs, and college fraternities/sororities would chuck down a beer or other alcoholic beverage as a joke to salute Gold Rush. It became a popular beguilement in many areas of the country and the butt of law enforcement officers, truckers and other professionals' jokes. It has gotten to the point of such ridiculousness that Chris had been very resigned about it and expressed that discontentment to me as well as to other members of Gold Rush.

****

Expletives

Notwithstanding the use of the word "freaking", Discovery wanted to add saltiness to the show by pretending that Todd and his men used expletives; they censored the crew post filming. Todd and his crew objected to that. They had no control over final editing, a process that took place after shooting commenced and before the footage was submitted for broadcasting. It totally distorted Todd and his men's testimony before the broadcast just for the sake of ratings.

****

Thurb' Obsession

I once overheard Jim say to Todd, "I can't talk publicly and what role can I have in Gold Rush?" In other words, much like everyone else's plight, what do I have to do to not sell my soul?

****

Bullied

Kato teaches self defense to Todd's boys. In the spirit of Bruce Lee, he taught actual fighting techniques to contract or expand when the moment of need arises. We had a few brief moments in Alaska. For example, I taught a few extrication techniques when they were confronted by a superior force. It is hoped that Todd's kids would want to continue to learn martial arts through proper instruction for the love of acquiring knowledge and not for the unnecessary need of being picked on as children of celebrities.

****

Dakota Fred

Midway through the first season, Dakota Fred stepped onto the scene as the spokesperson representing the landowner where Todd was mining. He became the object of scorn, most notably from Greg and also from James (to a lesser degree). My first encounter with him took place at a Haines civic function where Todd was asked to speak. Todd was preempted by the appearance of Dakota Fred, who attempted to take center stage. When Fred issued Todd a friendly verbal joust, he politely refused to be drawn in and verbalized to me: "Who invited him here?" After many autographs and photos were taken of Todd and his crew, we departed the function and headed for dinner at their usual downtown hangout. We began to look at the bill of fare when all of a sudden, Dakota Fred came in and sat down next to me, grinning wildly. He proceeded to order his dinner. I was very uncomfortable, a sentiment surely shared by others at the dinner table. Even though we ate quickly, Dakota Fred departed before us and left us his tab.

****

Hidden Gold

Based on the ten-year average of approximately 50,000 ounces of placer gold produced in the Yukon each year, how could Todd's group alone yield nearly 2% of the total in one year? Notwithstanding the industry's sophisticated technology that's employed by several major mining companies with many more years of proven experience, the question must be raised as to the veracity in the amount of gold reportedly produced from Todd and/or Parker. This can be described as the crux of the entire show. In the After Show itself, the executive producer described the amount of gold produced by everyone was just a "representation" and not the actual gold that was mined and formed into ingots on the show.

Under the Placer Mining Act 386 KB, Yukon, it levies a royalty on all gold shipped from the Yukon for export, whether it be in the form of gold dust as mined or bars. The royalty is computed at the rate of 2.5% of the value of the gold, or at such lesser rate as may be fixed by the Commissioner-in-Council.

Without revealing each day's production, Todd kept his men in the dark. By not reporting your production, benefits do arise for certain benefactors. For example, up until June 2015, McDonald's Corporation was the last fast food chain to report their weekly sales production. What about Todd's?

****

Jack's Mourning

Every pet owner, especially one with "man's best friend", is undeniably a friend indeed. Jack loses Blue, who was his very beloved companion of so many years. After being rescued from the animal shelter, the dogs truly become more trusted and lovable. I found mine there, too. I certainly enjoyed Blue's company as well.

After Jack's back operation a couple of years ago, he recognizes the pain he had to endure while working hard on Gold Rush. Needless to say, Jack can certainly empathize with James' health condition better than anyone else and can appreciate the sacrifice he made in working with Todd's team.

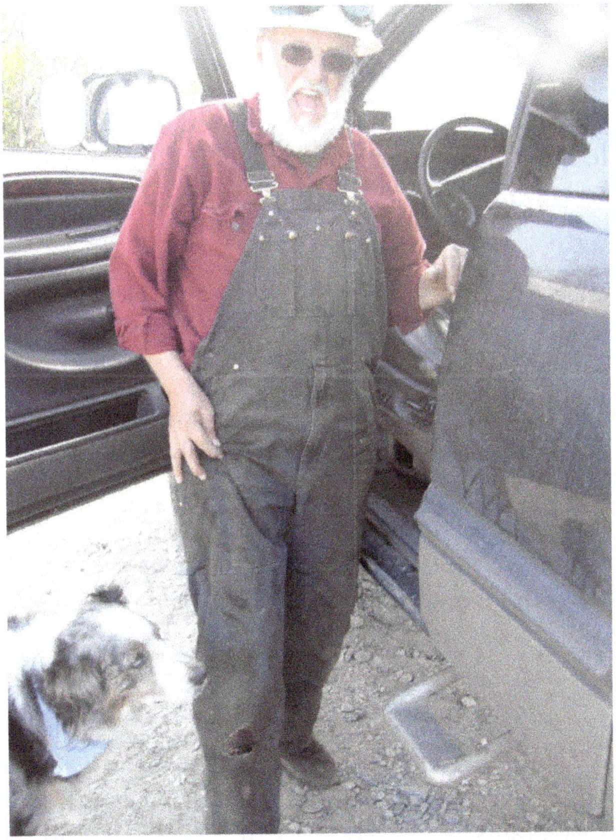

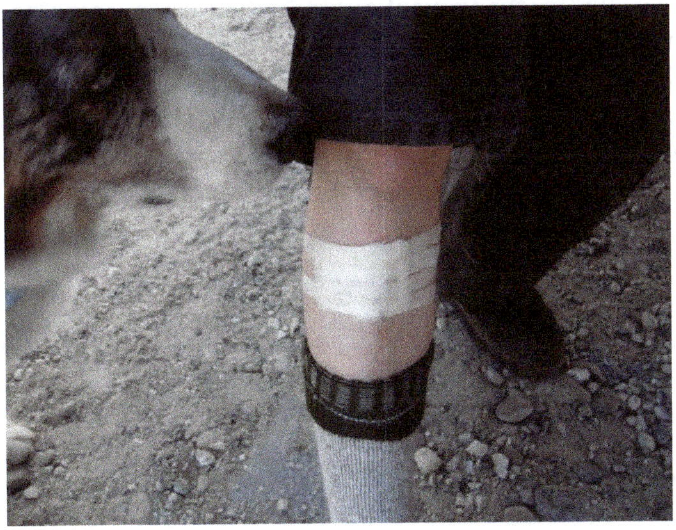

****

Chris' Hearing

When it was announced that Todd wanted to use season four as a new throwaway season for his serial strategy and move to a new mining location, Chris replied, "Ghana in Africa" when he could have meant to say Guyana in South America. Whether it was mispronounced by Todd or misheard by Chris, I wonder whether it was a Freudian slip on someone's behalf?

****

Drugs

James was accused of taking drugs. So was Todd. Unless you classify prescribed medication in the form of muscle relaxants and pain killers as drugs, then James is guilty like many of us. The notion of Todd using drugs came up only when he was sniffling in one of the After Show episodes. I and no one else has even seen him take a cough drop. Interestingly, Todd has introduced me to a white substance in which we both have become addicted to - "Ice Breakers", sugar-free mints. Hey, product placement?

****

Gertie's

One of the best places that we went for evening meals was at Diamond Tooth Gertie's Gambling Hall, Canada's oldest casino and, the Yukon's most visited attraction. Like most (if not all) restaurants in Dawson City, it served alcoholic beverages. The food was very good, especially for the value it gives. In the early evening, the show featured dancers prominent to the gold rush era of the late 1890's. As the evening progressed with different shows, clothing became scantier and ratings passed PG. One early evening, all the cast members and RAW crew members attended a dinner and show in the VIP section of the second floor to thank Todd for his leadership. Everyone, except Todd and Kato (who each abstains from alcoholic beverages), appeared livid when Dave acquiesced and appeared on stage. Nothing wrong happened but I've decided against publishing cameo shots of that night.

In the late evenings (around and past midnight) at the Gold Rush RV campground, I usually stay up and peer through the rear window of Jack's RV where I "sleep" and watch over everyone's trailer. Occasionally (for fun), I shine my million candle power spotlight on their faces as they walk past me and get a few chuckles.

****

Who's Taking the Photo?

In the infamous group photo of Jim, Dave, Chris, James, Todd, Kato and Jack, who was taking the picture? Several copies of this photo are hanging on people's walls or sitting on their desks with an inscription written on them. Many surmised that Greg was taking the photo since he was not in the shot himself. I never commented on that point because, as mentioned previously, Todd sent him home and Discovery portrayed Greg returning to Oregon to find immediate, gainful employment so that food can be put on the table.

****

The Rebel

We have already discussed that James has had enough of inefficiency and wants to make their gold mining more productive. Chris quits when he was cornered and interrogated by Todd, et al. Greg departs with a bad taste in his mouth and changed horses (employers), so to speak. Could Jimmy Dorsey have been the original progenitor of Gold Rush rebels? As first year participant of the ground breaking Gold Rush show, Dorsey (as told by other members of the show) was rumored to have withheld some or all of his medication and "let loose" as a result. Needless to say, he got into trouble and ratings went up. It was also reported by the other members that he wanted to get into every shot while the camera was rolling.

****

Loyalty

At what price will loyalty cost each of Todd's men? Once friends since high school, they no longer say anything; there is an occasional wave or a friendly hand gesture even though they just live across the street from each other. Some have been bribed with extraordinary gifts. Others have been pushed aside over a set of clothes.
Friendship synonyms=comrade, chum, confidant, backer, ally, associate

****

Hard Rock

Not the kind James was accustomed to. Once placer gold mining comes to an end in this area, hard rock mining will have arrived. Hard rock mining extracts veins of gold and silver from solid rock which is underneath the placer deposits. Claims are now being staked for the best ground to dynamite with explosives. Could this be Todd or Discovery's latest show? If Todd chooses not to pursue this venture for himself, then it would certainly promise to be a blast for a new series somewhere else.

****

Discovery's Valley of Fire & Resurrecting Dredging

Once out in the gold fields, the original Klondike miners who only used tools fashioned from local lumber worked on open cuts like Todd or chose the more popular method of going underground. The old prospectors sunk a shaft along the pay streaks. Before they can drift alongside them, the miners had to thaw through the permafrost, an endeavor that Todd failed to adequately do in the second season.

Without even a working wash plant available at their disposal, the mining season was quickly passing them by. The frozen ground of winter was slowly turning into miserable slush; the result was that dozers and excavators were dangerously slipping and sliding without good footing. It made for good TV drama though. Every mining company in the Yukon region was well underway mining and moving mountains of earth by the hour. Learning from this mistiming mistake, Todd sent Greg, Dave and Chris much earlier (mid-spring) the following season, months before the rest of his crew arrived.

Nearing the end of the mining season and still targeting for a spectacular 1,000 ounce mining season (ten times the previous year's yield), Discovery wanted to show Todd making a last ditch effort to attain that lofty goal by thawing the onset of frozen ground with fire, a technique used a century earlier to thaw permafrost with wood fires. Jack suggested that what worked then certainly would work now and executed it as such.

At the very turn of the twentieth century, steam replaced wood fire to thaw which then gave way to bucket-line dredging, the last major mining process before the eventual introduction of heavy equipment that we see today.

Described as huge caterpillars, dredge tailings from the likes of Dredge #4, the largest wooden hull dredge in North America, punctuate the entire landscape as far as the eye can see - a roaming legacy until the early 1960's and resurrected for Gold Rush a half century later.

A KLONDIKE DREDGE

1. GOLD BEARING GRAVEL
2. BUCKET EXCAVATOR
3. REVOLVING SCREEN
4. GOLD SAVING SLUICE
5. TAILINGS STACKER
6. DREDGE PIVOT POINT
7. MASTER CONTROL ROOM
8. FLOATING BARGE
9. SELF-DUG DREDGE POND
10. TAILINGS- (WASHED GRAVEL)

1. GRAVIER AURIFÈRE
2. EXCAVATEUR À GODETS
3. TAMIS ROTATIF
4. CANAL DE RÉCUPÉRATION DE PÉPITES
5. CONVOYEUR DE TERRIL
6. POINT DE PIVOTAGE DU DRAGUEUR
7. SALLE DE CONTRÔLE CENTRAL
8. BARGE
9. BASSIN DE DRAGUAGE
10. TERRIL (GRAVIER LAVÉ)

JAMES DISABLED

James' auto accident resulted in permanent injury. There was no way to correct the problem, there were only ways to manage it. The irrevocably ruptured discs, disjointed vertebrae and central nervous system disorder caused significant inflammation and constant muscle spasms – there was no cure, there was only some level of pain control.

Oral and intravenous pain medication is temporal and only masks the issue. At the initial time of the accident, surgery was technologically in its infancy when compared with today's advances.

The financial amount offered in legal settlement (compounded after legal expenses) was woefully too weak to support the costs of long-term "recovery". (I wish we had known each other before Gold Rush so that I could have referred him to some of the best law firms in the country). Having said this, this did not deter James' attempts to resume a normal life. No longer capable of a professional career with GM, James attempted to not only survive but to thrive the best way he could under the circumstances.

When the opportunity of Gold Rush became available, James had to weigh it from all sides - physically and mentally. Carpe diem, but with precaution. He wanted to only be an adviser telling the other men how to perform the mechanical side of the operation. Any physical exertion - whether lifting his arm or moving a leg or a slight twist to the hips - could trigger spasms lasting for hours. Anyone who can tolerate such unrelenting pain must have had the ability to control it mentally, otherwise it's just plain torture!

Temporary pain control through medication is very expensive and only masks briefly. Sometimes, it is hoped the medication would reduce inflammation and cut the vicious circle of spasms. James had no choice but to tough it out - not on a weekly basis, not even on a daily basis, and certainly not even on a minute by minute basis. It was a moment by moment basis.

Any person with a back injury that was just a quarter of the damage that James had can identify the excruciating pain one must endure. James told me that the only relief he oftentimes resorted to was to cry himself into oblivion and bite into a piece of leather or wood. James was no cry baby in any sense of the word. He didn't complain about his misfortune. James accepted it and tried to move on with his life the best way he could.

Looking back retrospectively, the work asked of him in season one appears inappropriate and demonstrates outright abuse for the sake of television sensationalism.

As shown on Gold Rush, James received medical assistance on the East Coast. They offered those services pro bono since he had no financial means to pay for it. What was not shown or disclosed was the fact that it consisted of procedures that offered "longer-term" temporary pain relief (we're talking about weeks). Again, physical exertion exacerbated his condition and actually compounded his well-being. James did what he had to do to help the cause - he did not want to let his friends down since they depended on him.

Through medical records and examination, the Social Security Administration rendered James' physical condition as permanently disabled and he thus received financial assistance.

JAMES REVISITED

Todd paid $1,000 per person per month in season one, to our understanding. In the second season, Discovery paid nominal salaries to the cast members. Everyone had to secure their own or someone's agent or deal directly with Discovery. After paying for Canadian taxes, salaries were further reduced by federal, state and/local deductions; this led to James owing the IRS significant back taxes.

Up until James' stroke and passing, he endured significant pressure in meeting his debt obligation. He worried over the possible seizure of his physical property where he was living in Redmond, Oregon. As a result, he pretty much stayed on his property 24/7 until he could get relief. I wouldn't say he was a prisoner of his own making but at least he tried to resolve his issue like any other problems he encountered. It was difficult for him just to meet the tax payment schedule, let alone the rent. James would not ask for financial assistance from his friends. He was too proud to do so.

The very first time before I arrived to meet him at his new residence, I called for us to rendezvous at a convenient location - Walmart. With a hearty handshake, I told him to grab a shopping cart also and we each went racing down the aisles picking up stuff that he needed (food and other necessities).

    The property where he lived had been neglected and rundown. James said that it required significant overhauling. When I first visited him, I remarked about how nice the house was. In exchange for low monthly leased rent, James made significant improvements. He told me that it was originally two old trailer homes. I said, "Don't pull my leg." James insisted that it was. He showed me pictures of the property before he improved it. He told me that it was almost totally rebuilt from the ground up. Hard to believe, but true. Due to the lack of a direct water supply, water had to be brought onto the property on a regular basis and drained into a large holding tank. Conservation was definitely on the order.

    James took me on a tour of his property and it really had a lot of potential for remodeling and new construction. The property itself seemed to be the perfect location to set up shop for not just mechanical work but also filming, research and development, new housing (for me), a music recording studio and heavy equipment and shipping. It already had a loading dock set up.

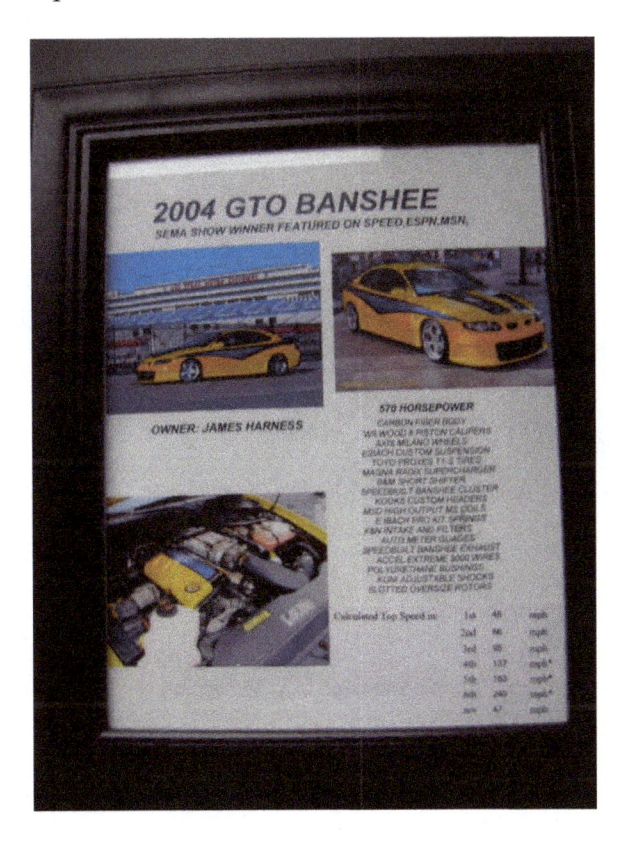

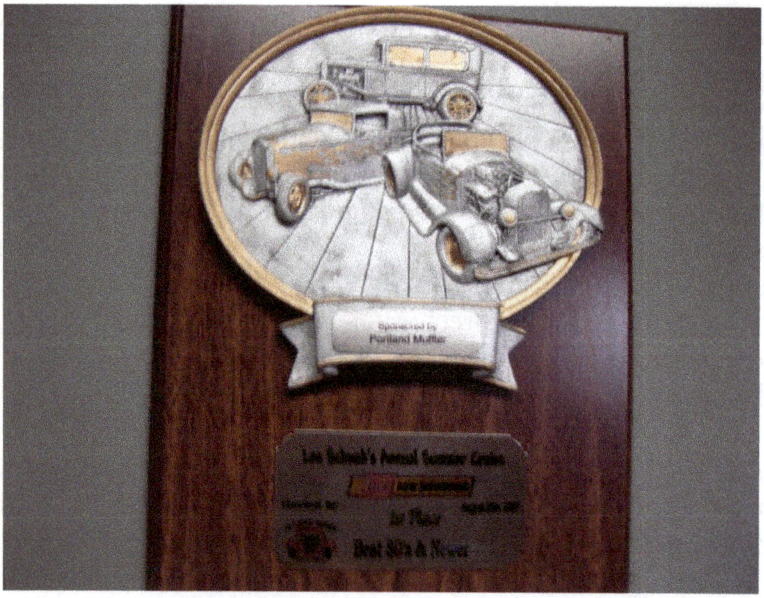
Sponsored by
Portland Muffler

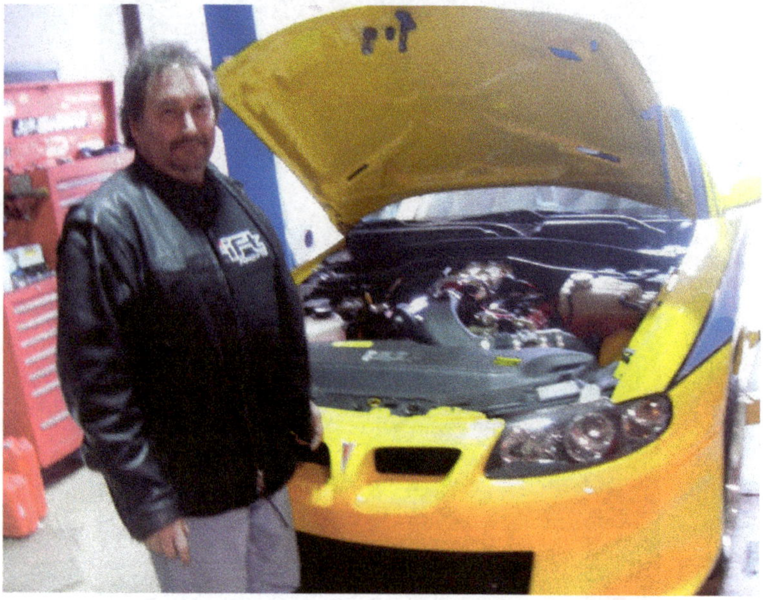

We went back into his home and he introduced me to his "little" puppy, who was at least 150 pounds - a very friendly and devoted companion. James was very happy and proud of him. Before heading out to dinner, James brought me into a large building where he stored his valuables. He thumbed through a box and handed me his entire first year of gold given to him by Todd and Jack.

Overwhelmed, I thanked him saying, "You can't part with this. You earned it a hundred times over. James, you literally gave your blood, sweat and tears for this."

James said, "Yep. That's why I'm giving it to you."

I said to myself, "How in the world can you respond to that?

Still with a sense of humor, James said, "Kato, I'll even give you the shirt off my back" and hands me the following.

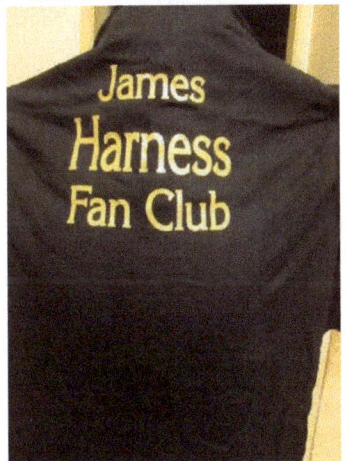

With that, it was dinner time. At the dinner table, I asked him why he put so much time and effort behind this rental property.

James said, "This property has a lot of potential and room and I want it to be my final home if I can arrive at a deal with the landlord."

I asked him why not move and pull stakes somewhere closer to me so we can work better together. Until that time, I relied on James for a lot of help, including plans to film on different continents. He was definitely integral to our mutual business plans. Despite this, James kindly but emphatically declined. His reason, "I want to be close to my children - they mean more to me than anything else in the world."

Our last supper – last photo of James alive

REMEMBERING

With a heavy heart traveling back down from Redmond, Oregon, I couldn't stop thinking of James and how I could have done something before he left this world. Maybe when many commanders, noncoms, or just fellow soldiers have this guilty feeling when one of their own gets killed, you ask yourself why you should be allowed to live. This proverbial guilt trip comes to me all the time and consumes me like I should have done something differently. In my case, I should have come sooner - at least a week upon learning from him that he had just suffered a stroke; should I have sent more money for medicine, accompany him to the hospital or bring him down to Stanford - anything to help?

In more than one phone conversation, James kept joking to me not to come because of his discolored, purple face - it was a result of him falling down face forward. I said "Don't be foolish. Look at my face, and I didn't fall face forward", as we both laughed.

James was embarrassed with his appearance so I relented by telling him that I would come a few more days later. He and I then said goodbye until next week.

Others comforted me and many offered their bits of wisdom. All could not relieve the pain. Instead of the last resort, we should always go to Him first. We can always turn to Him anytime. God is the author of life and we cannot fathom the reasons for calling James or loved ones home. I mentioned to James not long before his stroke that when we are absent from the body, i.e., physically die, we are present with the Lord (2 Corinthians 5:6-8). There is no time lapse, not even a fraction of a nanosecond waiting in limbo. When we see Him face to face, we should actually look forward to it in joy. The only sadness is for those left behind who miss the dearly departed. But even that will be temporary until we should meet again, soon. With that comes comfort that is real. I'm sure James recognized that as he really did look more joyful and sounded happier when I saw him the next time.

If James could speak to us right now, he may say:

> "I'm all right now, in the best place that anyone can be. My pain is forever gone and never to be remembered. See you soon."

HOW I KILLED JAMES

Since James' passing, I tormented myself in writing this. Not because of guilt, but to reveal the truth. I'll let you the reader decide.

The week I was supposed to fellowship with my brother, he suffered a stroke. James calls me to wait for a little while but that didn't really change our plans. I actually wanted to come right up that very moment when he called me about his stroke. James was kind of laughing or amused with embarrassment that when he fell forward, his entire face became black and blue or purple. I told him that I didn't care what he looked like but he said that he was all right. So I delayed my trip with him for a little while longer.

When I was ready to come up, my car broke down and James sounded a little disappointed. He told me what to do to fix it. Then he wanted to resume the Audi A6 project for me. It was a salvage title vehicle which suffered front-end damage when it struck a deer. After replacing the bumper, he needed to paint it. As a professional, James wanted it to be in absolutely the best condition it could be before turning it over to me. Up until that time, James was under extreme pressure from the IRS to pay taxes owed from the Gold Rush TV show. Under his confidence, we decided that he would sell to me both the Audi and the GMC dually pickup used in the trek to Alaska and the Yukon. The truck had very little mechanical needs to be performed before it had to be sold. The Audi was to be totally refurbished to its original condition. I think he needed money for medicine immediately. I'll continue to send him payments in the meanwhile. A day or two later, James calls me asking,

"Whether his brother Frank in Washington (state) can have the truck for his new line of work?"

Without hesitation, I acquiesced that his brother's needs far outweigh mine - family first, I said. We were going to use the truck and camper for another television project that he was going to head up for me. James was under heavy pressure from the IRS and got an impression that they would seize his personal property to pay for taxes; I told him not to worry and to not push himself physically in readying the Audi. I don't know if he felt unduly obligated to get the car ready for me as soon as possible. Knowing James, that may have put added pressure on him. Lastly, James confided that he worried in leaving his Redmond property unguarded for almost any extended period of time. I told him that we'll resolve that issue when I come up. The "barn" doors were not fully secured, the adjoining sauna room has had an unwanted intruder recently and the property was pretty much left wide open by the sheer fact of its openness. The point was not to worry. To date, I don't know how much stress I could have obviated by coming sooner. I still feel guilty that I should have ignored James' request to delay my coming. Because I had already accompanied him to some of his medical appointments in the past, I was acquainted with some of his personal medical needs and was aware of his limitations with respect to his spinal injuries. I just feel guilty in making him physically do what was beyond his limit. I should have helped him in that car renovation.

Another thing to reiterate is that I shouldn't have sent money - I should have delivered it immediately and rendered whatever aid I could. I should have gone up there ASAP. However, I went a few days later and things could be different today, at least in my mind.

For those who have served in the military and suffered combat fatalities under your command, there is a sense of guilt that you carry around your neck because you're still alive.

I know about Monday morning quarterbacking. We talked about going to Stanford Medical Center, the country's best in practically every area of medicine. I wanted to take James there - just like Chris Doumitt - and do whatever it takes to get him back into some reasonable form of normal, permanent pain-free living. If not permanent, at least longer intermittent pain-free living. The "operation" that James had done on a charitable basis back East was unsuccessful and only gave temporary relief, he said. Maybe James worried about paying for everything himself. Even though he didn't have the money, he also didn't want charity. I told him that he should look at it from the stand point of it being an advance against future work to be completed later. Only near the end did he find that to be a palatable solution. Near-term plans were on the broiler to meet with Stanford's department heads, those who teach and supervise all medical procedures to their best students.

When I met with Greg and his wife in Palm Springs not too long after James' passing, I learned of Greg's great concern for James' soul. He was almost begging God to allow James know of Christ's gift of eternal life. I tried to comfort Greg at that moment but I now agree with him that I too share some of the responsibility in being a better witness of Him to James. This guilt will definitely (and should) not leave me.

I appreciated Jack's invitation to ride with him and Blue in his Dodge to Alaska. But because of James' salvation, we decided that I should ride with James. That was my primary reason for riding with him to Alaska. As I look back, we can expect good things to result from our discussions. In other words, I remember very vividly what we talked about.

Beyond James' love for music composition and performing, he asked a lot of questions about life, its origins and what the future holds. He definitely had questions answered from both a supporting basis as well as from a living faith. This, at least, gives me comfort. There is one certainty and that is God is the author of life, no matter what mere man can say and do.

Here is something that helped James find strength each day, both physically and mentally:

"But we have this treasure in jars of clay to show that this all surpassing power is from God and not from us.
We are hard pressed on every side, but not crushed;
perplexed, but not in despair;
persecuted, but not abandoned;
struck down, but not destroyed.
Therefore, we do not lose heart.
Though outwardly we are wasting away, yet inwardly we are being renewed day by day.
For our light and momentary troubles are achieving for us an eternal glory that far outweighs them all.
So we fix our eyes not on what is seen, but on what is unseen.
For what is seen is temporary, but what is unseen is eternal."

2 Corinthians 4: 7-17

FUNERAL DAY

      James' son, Adam (the spitting image of a young James), invited me to attend the service with all the family members. This invitation was offered after I returned from James' home in Redmond. I was honored and really wanted to attend and share my experiences, good times, plans and dreams of James with the family. I had a veritable album of photos shot over the 4 years we had together and offered to hand many of these out for keepsakes.

      I was in San Diego attending the annual Comic-Con and was wrapping up my obligations and fulfilling my responsibilities for the weekend there and had planned to drive non-stop to the Portland area for the service the following morning. It was around 5 P.M. when the freeway became congested just outside the city. I encountered heavy downtown traffic and meandered north on the 5. Three plus hours later and less than 75 miles north, traffic grinded to a halt outside Anaheim and moved at a snail's pace to a screeching stop again near Los Angeles. I saw a CHP (California Highway Patrol) unit parked on the right shoulder and went to it to learn that a man was perched over a freeway overpass five miles up threatening suicide. With every lane and exit jammed, I asked the officer how I can get through to Oregon. He told me to go on the shoulder, double back, take this other road and jump back onto the 5 (Interstate). I said, "You gotta be kidding!" but he was serious. Realizing my predicament, he escorted me around and beyond this impasse. Back on the 5, I saw over the horizon a veritable sea of red taillights leading up to the "grapevine" (20 miles further). I immediately calculated the number of miles to reach Oregon and found that I didn't have enough hours to make it. Right then and there I thought I was providentially hindered and immediately conveyed my regrets for my inability to get out of Southern California in time. I apologized to Adam. (I pulled over to the shoulder to make the call). I plan to present to all the family members photos of James that I took at the Sandy Airport, on the trek to Alaska and the Yukon, at Dawson City, at the mining sites, at home in Redmond and candid shots taken while working out for future projects.

Some personal items of interest as well as items from the Gold Rush TV show were to be exhibited and given away.

In apologizing and asking for forgiveness, Adam graciously thanked me anyway for trying and said, "We'll talk later." A few days after the service, I called Adam. He said that there was not a single dry eye at the chapel service. Everyone who gave a testimony of James couldn't hold back the tears while trying to smile at the same time. They proudly stood up and spoke about their experiences and love for James.

This is what I wanted to say if I had attended the service personally:

Thank you Adam and family members for inviting me. None of you would know who I am unless James mentioned that I became his brother in more ways than one. We enjoyed each other's company at the Sandy Airport as we prepared for the second season of Gold Rush. I became his apprentice in getting all the trucks ready for departure; we secured all the necessary equipment and supplies, coordinated logistics and bought and serviced a new truck for Jim Thurber. He introduced me to Harbor Freight. In other words, James made time in helping others. As we departed for Alaska, we listened to music that he composed and he seriously planned to assemble a new band. This idea, as well as others we discussed, were by no means fly by night stories but realistic, accurate and well-organized and structured like any professional business. Why am I saying this? To demonstrate that James had a business acumen and had a lot to look forward to in life. He told me that he really wanted to help all his family members. James had a lot of living to do. Despite his physical infirmities, it did not sway him from planning the things that he was most capable of doing. James told me of his auto accident and his difficult climb back to some semblance of normalcy. Our conversation naturally turned to the subject matter of life once we have exhausted our physical well-being, i.e., pass on. Among the many areas we discussed from the Scriptures, I pointed out that:

> "Now we know that if the earthly tent we live in is destroyed, we have a building from God, an eternal house in heaven, not built by human hands. Meanwhile we groan, longing to be clothed with our heavenly dwelling, because when we are clothed, we will not be found naked. For while we are in this tent, we groan and are burdened, because we do not wish to be unclothed but to be clothed with our heavenly dwelling, so that what is mortal may be swallowed up by life. Now it is God who has made us for this very purpose and has given us the Spirit as a deposit guaranteeing what is to come. Therefore we are always confident and know that as long as we are at home in the body we are away from the Lord. So we make it our goal to please Him, whether we are at home in the body or away from it."
>
> 2 Corinthians 5: 1-9

In other words, I said to James: absent from the body (physical death) means you'll be present with the Lord, immediately. No limbo nor time spanned, no waiting. Instantly, faster than the blinking of your eye.

> And Jesus says, "In my Father's house are many rooms; if it were not so, I would have told you. I am going there to prepare a place for you.
> And if I go and prepare a place for you, I will come back and take you to be with me that you also may be where I am. You know the way to the place where I am going."
> Thomas said to him, "Lord, we don't know where you are going, so how can we know the way?"
> Jesus answered, "I am the way and the truth and the life. No one comes to the Father except through me."
>
> John 14: 2-6

Sitting on the passenger side of his truck, I looked at James and saw that he was smiling and tearing a little bit. James said that was reassuring. I couldn't agree more. I said to him that no matter what lies ahead in our lives, you can bank on knowing where we will spend eternity by placing our trust in Him. James nodded and we kept rolling.

UNFULFILLED PLANS

James and I were in the process of making serious plans for filming; several projects were in varying stages of completion. During one long night in the Sandy Airport Lodge before our departure for the Alaskan trip, I wrote treatment for about one hundred television shows. I still have the treatments stashed away. I know at least some of them are good since they have already been brought to the attention of TV executives. James and I had a long, planned agenda in place before he had the stroke.

In the midst of suffering the stroke, James told me his daughter was there to help. Because stroke medication exhausted his finances, I called and informed him that another payment was forthcoming. James thanked me. On the phone, he spoke with a little hesitancy. James assured me of his undying devotion for me and said he had to talk quicker since money on his cell phone was nearing empty. I told him to keep a stiff upper lip as I was preparing to leave shortly to visit him. James said, "Hurry up so we can go to have some fun at the firing range." Without realizing what the full extent was, I quickly said, "No. Let's work first and then play later (my typical response). James kind of laughed. I told him that we are all praying for you to have a speedy and full recovery as soon as possible and to call me for whatever reason. In conclusion, I told him that I loved him as my own brother.

When driving up I-5, I was visualizing the fun we were going to have. Besides eating out and having a blast (at the range), we had a long agenda to work on. I wanted to stay at least a week or two. I remembered when James suggested last month to go gold mining in central Oregon instead of Australia or some other exotic locale for filming; I finally realized that it was because he didn't want to be far from his family. This theme finally hits home.

As I was crossing into Oregon, I called James but there was no pickup, only a recording on his cell phone. I thought James was indisposed, or worse case, back in the hospital. I arrived in the late afternoon and parked outside the gate because there was no pick up to his cell phone again. James told me in the last conversation that only a few minutes remained on his phone. Walking hurriedly at a brisk pace around the bend, I began to call out James' name. I was really anxious to greet my brother-in-arms. I didn't see his truck parked in the front so I thought he stepped out.

Suddenly, a younger man appeared and I introduced myself. I couldn't believe my own eyes when this handsome gentleman introduced himself as James' son - a veritable spitting image of a younger James. Adam then told me that his father just past on recently.

Like a ton of bricks falling on me, I dropped to the ground and landed on the porch steps. Holding my lowered head with my arms, I finally broke my own shocking silence by saying to him: "He is in heaven now in the presence of God and his physical pain is gone forever."

All I could give to them (Adam's sister was there too) were words of assurance and whatever assistance they needed. Adam thanked me. It was time for me to travel home with a heavy heart.

I know James is in God's hands but I still missed him. One thing is for sure, it will only be a short while until I see him again. Little did I know that our last conversation a few days ago centered around eternity.

PALM SPRINGS

Rather than phoning, I unequivocally drove to Palm Springs to convey a message from James Harness to Greg Remsburg. Prior to this, I was about to meet with James at his home in Redmond for a week or two of work (mostly regarding the television strategy we had been planning for several shows). Upon arrival, James' son told me of his passing. In anticipation of James' funeral, I contacted Chris and he informed Greg, who in turn notified the RAW television crew who informed Todd.

After picking up Greg and his wife at the airport car rental where they had just returned from a meeting with his agent in Los Angeles, I settled them down at their nice resort and we went to the "best" restaurant we could find under the circumstances - a (Gay Pride) celebration and parade was taking place in the heart of downtown at the same time we're looking for the shortest line to get food. After ordering our lunch, I conveyed James' message to Greg.

James wanted Greg to know that he was the only original cast member to wish him well after leaving Gold Rush. James thought that it was very important for Greg to know this as he told me to convey it personally if the situation ever arose. I have too much respect for Greg (and James of course) to not carry out my duty and obligation to each of them.

Greg was heartbroken, speechless and visibly moved after telling him of this. After holding back in this painful, emotional time, we each reminisced the good times we shared with James. Greg was extremely concerned with James' standing with the Lord when he asked about his life after the Gold Rush years. Realizing that only God can save souls, I tried to comfort Greg by saying that God will do whatever it takes to bring James to Himself. Like a true friend, Greg was deeply concerned as to whether or not James knew the Lord. I told Greg that instead of riding with Jack to Alaska, (where two military guys can talk for endless hours all the way up there), it would be a good idea to share, witness and fellowship with James while riding up. In addition to the myriad of subjects discussed, he asked a lot of questions about history and the Scriptures.

After James left the show, we had the best fellowship both while together as well as when we talked on the phone at least once a week. To divert the seriousness of the situation, I recounted the many untold contributions that James made to the success of Todd's mission/show including the servicing of all the vehicles going up to Alaska, locating, purchasing and servicing Jim's new truck and maintaining and repairing everyone's trucks during the years on the show. No need to remind Greg of the sacrifice of James on the show itself.

To further lessen the sadness in our lunch meeting, Greg and I recounted James' sense of humor; after suffering his stroke he didn't want me to see his black, blue and purple face after falling face forward. James did not want his neighbors to think voodoo was being practiced outside of the New Orleans Mardi Gras. That brought smiles to the table. Finally, I told Greg that beyond James' technical skills (of which I needed so integrally for my work), I told him that it would set me back considerably to find several (irreplaceable) replacements. Lastly, I said that I'm going to miss James very much and that I loved him as my own brother. I'm sure that Greg shares the same sentiment.

After lunch and dessert, I insisted and Greg acquiesced to another entree. I returned them back to their resort and left.

While driving back I remembered that I should have thanked Greg for standing up and setting the record straight, as you might say. When I first got word to Chris to return my phone call, I asked him to inform Todd and others of James' passing. It was learned that Greg alerted the RAW crew members to gather around him as he offered a tribute to James Harness. Except for Chris and Greg, most if not all the RAW crew members of the Parker team have never worked with any of the other cast members. Greg, while not denigrating the recent passing of Blue, emphasized the greater significance of the role James played in the first two seasons of Gold Rush and credited him with the success the show now enjoys. Greg cited James not only for his technical skills in their initial mining operation, but acknowledged his sacrifices of mind and body in bringing Gold Rush to fruition.

I strongly believe that the foregoing testimony is a further testament of Greg's strong character and something that will not go without recompense.

"I know James is smiling at Greg."

Palm Springs 2014

EVERYBODY WRITES

    This is what they would honestly say if each wrote a book about their experiences of being in Gold Rush. The big question is what would they do AFTER Gold Rush is over.

Todd

-How and why did I ever conceive of Gold Rush?

-The enormity in planning for such a venture.

-Why and where did I pick up these guys to work for me?

-Should I share my good fortune with some, all or none?

-The hours in praying for it to happen favorably, or for God to bless it?

-The money needed to get it off the ground and what it took to keep it going.

-How much do I need to pay these guys?

-What price glory in exchange for compromising my convictions?

-Can I keep these guys in line or turn them loose?

-Was RAW my best pick or the only production company who wanted to take a chance with an amateurish video produced by (Todd) a rookie?

-The agony and begging it took to get it (show) off the ground.

-Can I work with the Discovery Channel?

-How long do I have to put up with the people that Discovery keeps sending to Sandy and the Yukon?

-Is my legacy worth all of this, or should I just shoot for the moon?

-Can I trust Discovery after they decided to put all of these other new characters in MY show - Fred, Parker, Tony, _____?

-How does it feel to be relegated to be second in the show, at least in terms of gold production?

-How does it feel knowing that your gold mining concept was spun off into genres of alternate gold and Alaskan shows on Discovery and other cable networks?

-I'm losing control of the show, where is it leading to?

-This "bleeping" sound Discovery puts in is misleading the intentions and character of the men and the show.

-How much do I have to give in order to keep the show going?

-I've said a lot of things that I shouldn't have.

-Should I take what Discovery wants to pay me or take less?

-I am doing whatever it takes in order to get what I want done to make my show.

-How much more staging do I have to make in order to keep it going?

-Ratings are beginning to slide.

-Should I take the money and succumb to Discovery's pressure in dropping BATTLEGROUND and other projects?

- Everyone knows the perception of how difficult I am to work with. So am I employable later or would anyone else in TV take a serious chance on me?

- In other words, am I still exploitable?

- Should I dare divulge my health to the world, or keep it private?

- How do (or should) I need to explain my actions?

- Do others think I'm selling them out?

- Going on strike certainly works. Everyone got their timely salary payments, food and equipment. What's next?

- Can I still look myself in the mirror?

- Will God forgive me?

- How much am I accountable to Him?

- Will it be worth it all when it's over?

- Is Gold Rush capable of getting my (God's) message across?

- Gold Rush cost me dearly, would I do it again?

- Kato, what's a Kato?

Jack

- Should I follow Todd's dream and go along with it?

- As a former Army soldier, I have to ask myself, "What price glory?"

- Can Todd pull this off another year?

- Can I muster the strength, despite my infirmities?

- Do I need to maintain the perception and continue this path for the sake of the show?

- How much do I need to put up with Discovery when they treat my son this way?

- When will this all end so I can get back to reality?

-I wish I could have done things differently.

-How much longer do I allow my family see me physically suffer?

-Do I care about TV ratings?

-Now that Blue is gone, can I continue to handle it without him at my side?

-Must I be subservient to Todd all the time (in front or behind the camera)?

-Shall I support Todd's endeavors in and out of Gold Rush?

-Must I lose the loyalty and support of my lifelong friends for the sake of this show?

-I liked James, Mike, Greg, Chris and the others.

-How do I answer to God?

-What if?

-Did I bite off more than I can chew?

-Glad I got Kato protecting me.

Greg

-Should I leap at this opportunity?

-Can I work with Todd?

-Can I work with Jack?

-The money I am going to make will really help my family.

-Will my family support me?

-Why doesn't my agent do a better job for me?

-How am I being portrayed in front of the camera? I know that others know me differently, especially my family - the most important thing in my life.

-Will I make it physically despite...?

-I need a better paying job.

-Do I need to submit to Todd? He's been my buddy since school days.

-Mom and Dad are not just watching me on TV.

-They (family) are more important now than ever before.

-I wish I didn't take this (Gold Rush) job.

-After beating up Dorsey, everyone now thinks I'm a bully.

-What do I need to say in front of the camera to make an impact or real difference in people's lives?

-How much pride must I need to swallow?

-What's in it for me?

-Besides God, who else is going to help and support my family?

-I can't stand Todd's dictates and orders.

-It's Todd's way or the highway.

-How much more do I need to do to endure working for Parker?

-I am going to write a book, guess what I am going to say?

-How did we ever wind up with Kato?

James

-Can I make it physically?

-Should I place my loyalty to Todd?

-Will Todd let me do my job?

-I know who I am and this show won't change me nor my convictions.

-Do I need this, especially after season one?

-If I go along with this for a second season, there's got to be change.

-Being on the show, will my family laugh or cry for me?

-Where's the beef (gold)?

-Must I play the role I was hired for or be myself?

-I know there is life after Gold Rush and it won't bother me for a second if I were to leave.

-Do I compromise my convictions for the sake of the show and ratings?

-I must speak up when no one else will.

-After a low gold production from the first season, there better not be another.

-Everyone I bump into wants the real scoop.

-Now that Todd has brought in Dave, I see the handwriting on the wall.

-Despite Todd's insistence, I know what it takes to make these expeditions work.

-I'm not a quitter, so why should Todd or Discovery make me look like one?

-Branded a thief forever.

-K-A-T-O

-Do I want to write a book? I know Kato will do a good job in writing what I want to say.

Jim

-What can I do in this show that Todd is proposing?

-How far can I trust Todd with my persona?

-Now that Gold Rush is a bona fide success, what can I get out of it?

-I hope my family doesn't mind me being portrayed as broke.

-After Gold Rush's glitter wears off, what kind of life will I have?

-The cost of bringing home the bacon.

-Will Todd bring me to the next adventure so long I remain faithful to his demands?

-Should I take a stand in the show, or go with the flow?

-I don't know why Todd wants me in the show since I'm not a great (content) speaker.

-Thurb, what kind of a name is that?

-So long as the gravy flows, I'm master of my destiny.

-I can___ look myself in the mirror each morning.

-Todd saying to Kato: "Thurb's only got a half of a box left of replacement mustaches in his RV."

-"You can always count on me (Jim, period). I'll (he'll) always be there when you need me (him)." (everybody!)

-Never going to let Kato borrow my truck again.

Chris

-When opportunity knocks, take it.

-What an opportunity to be on Gold Rush, even for a few episodes.

-Can Gold Rush give me a second career?

-My own TV show, like "Wounded Warriors"?

-Will Gold Rush provide me a platform to help troubled youths in Oregon and elsewhere?

-I got the TV bug and now I can't shake it off.

-I lost a lot of time when I helped Gold Rush, now it's time to help my family and others.

-Can Gold Rush rebound after slipping in the ratings the past season?

-I don't like what Todd is doing.

-I won't be Todd's scapegoat.

-What should I say to the audience when I'm leaving Gold Rush permanently?

-Should I return to Gold Rush and work for Parker?

-I know I can get the strength to endure physically, mentally and spiritually.

-ACTUAL question asked sincerely in the Yukon - "Kato, would you answer me one question, are you an a____."

Dave

-As a church leader, can I do this show?

-Can I follow Todd's leadership?

-Can I serve Him (Jesus) as my Lord in this show?

-Will I help or hurt my testimony by remaining in Gold Rush?

-Is Gold Rush important enough to get my message across?

-I am infected with the TV bug and know no cure?

-Accomplice to Todd, or was it real?

-I'm happy that my family and friends support me.

-Despite a few miscues, He was always there to pick me up.

-Forgiven before, now and forever.

-What an adventure Gold Rush was.

-I'm ___ glad Gold Rush is over, now it's time to get back to the real task at hand.

-"Kato, let go. I can't breathe."

The proverbial question each has to answer:

"Does the end justify the means?"

LINGERING ISSUES

According to Chris and Sharon, when I dropped by their house on _____ Boulevard, she said "James Harness was not a good worker . . . ."

"Jim Thurber always was around at the Sandy Airport to do work, such as cleaning, painting etc. to be near Todd, even though he lives in Portland", according to an observer. At the beginning of our first meeting, Jim said to me, "I want to open a soup kitchen for the homeless."

Todd gave four vials of gold to obtain investor interest. Yet this amount deprived them of achieving their 100 ounce target. In other words, I should be taking the blame for missing the elusive 100 ounce mark, not James Harness.

LAST PARAGRAPH

By bordering on the reality of facts in scripting incidents and events on Gold Rush, it will further erode the trust between Discovery Channel and its loyal television audience. This obviously will lead to lower viewership and declining corporate commercial revenue, ending of course, to a quick coup de grace. A return to its original thesis and genuineness will certainly earn the respect of audience sophistication and support in which the show claimed.

After the success of the first season (the highest TV ratings on Friday), what do you think will happen when Todd's creation is slowly taken away from him? Many more TV shows are mimicking the same and similar genre on Discovery and other cable channels. It's too bad that not very many real gold mining companies have the same opportunity to finance their operations by drawing funds from unlimited, deep (Discovery) pockets.

If it seems that we may be harsh in judging Todd's actions towards his men, his family and even the Discovery Channel executives, you may be right. Little did we know, Todd's motives were sincerely made with the intention of making a top rated television show. He had no prior experience in this industry and yet achieved the very pinnacle of his newly chosen profession. It's true, in making decisions which resulted in consequences leading to dramatic effect over reality, Todd succeeded in pioneering a new genre of adventure which has in turned branched out into new television series beyond Discovery's grasp. It takes a lot of inner strength to see this through and yet, strength certainly had to be drawn beyond his own. Without the rigid support of Jack and his family, Todd may have ended this a whole lot sooner. This "drive" cannot be diminished unless his motives are from above and not from below, i.e., a cause far greater than his very own.

From the beginning, Todd declared that their mission was to serve God in reaching souls. It is hoped that they do not lose sight of this or their entire Gold Rush production would crumble like a deck of cards precariously stacked. Notwithstanding this, you cannot run over your men that you've selected to be on the show nor disregard the common sense of duty and respect that each one deserves. Personal sacrifice doesn't always appear superficially; unintentionally as though it may seem, that is why Todd tries so hard. As the saying goes, unless you walk in his shoes, don't judge him at all and give him the benefit of the doubt. Without prior experience of real leadership (unlike most, like Jack, who have experienced such in the military), his baptism under fire was truly miraculous. On the job training can be deemed inexcusable.

SWAN SONG

What will Todd need to make season 8 a success? The burden is on him, not Parker nor Tony. It requires something spectacular or an event to ensure Todd and Gold Rush's survival. Some speculations:

1. Find the next biggest Mother Lode
2. Recover the largest gold nugget ever found
3. A very serious or fatal injury (caught on film)
4. A major conflict between team members
5. Incontrovertible controversy resolved

Todd has got to make it big this upcoming season. If Todd can't deliver the goods to resurrect declining ratings, one of three things will happen:

First, the season will run its course and be canceled or not renewed.

Second, Todd will be replaced, along with his crew, by another team.

Third, Todd would play second or third fiddle.

In any event, it's either boom or bust.

CONCLUSION

When you cut it up, trim the fat, dice it, what do you have? An unreal reality show.

Unless you film something in its entirety without need to stop for any reason (including bathroom breaks for the camera crew, not having the need to compensate the subjects for their time and not filming the subjects to the liking of editors), then it is safe to say that you have a legitimate reality show. The only difference is three to five million regular, loyal viewers. To hold their interest, you should demonstrate to the sophisticated audience a sincerity from the subjects you are filming. It is also wise for the channel to not contribute to the outcome of the show that is being televised. Otherwise, you have a well-scripted show that is not real.

Here is a clear example of what I am trying to say. Let's take a collegiate football game between West Point and the Naval Academy of Annapolis. Both are non-professional teams being played without the need for monetary interest - both schools are funded by federal taxes. The game is being played without the need for corporate sponsors nor for a pay-per-view-audience. The outcome, being watched in the stands of between 70-90,000 fans, is literally up in the air until the final gun is sounded after sixty minutes have been formally played. The football game has certified officiating throughout plus monitors in the booths for certain replays. Everyone on the playing field congratulates each other for a well-played sporting game, including coaching staffs. Without the undue influence of external forces that are banned (like cheating and gambling), the entire game cannot be construed as fair and real without these well-guarded parameters. Otherwise, it's no longer a real contest like it was intended to be.

So along the same lines, we can be entertained with a legitimate broadcast or entertained by an illegitimate broadcast claiming to be real. Therefore, based upon your definitions of what is real or not, you the viewer must decide where the boundary of reality should be. You must find your own comfort level between the extreme of watching a great rivalry or maybe "Hawaii Five-0" or "Blue Bloods". If you find the definitions of what is unreal claiming to be real distasteful, then you have the undaunted, mind-boggling task of deciding what every generation must face in life sooner or later - turn to another channel, or turn the TV off and write your own book.

$$$

Discovery grossed over $1 billion off of Gold Rush (Todd) alone and Todd doesn't really mind. He minds, however, the criticism that he gets from everyone including fans, supporters and followers. He told me that while we were at the Sandy Airport.

Setting himself as the bar to jump over, Todd's first season was truly a milestone.

Even Tom Selleck's "Blue Bloods" on CBS moved to a different day and time slot in order to keep running and not be canceled. When Gold Rush's season was completed, CBS reinserted "Blue Bloods" back to its former day and time.

For the second season, Todd succeeded in surpassing the glory of his inaugural one. However, he's loses his grip when new elements were brought in - two rival gold mining operators. This was done without Todd's knowledge. Compounding this was the introduction of a spinoff of Todd's Gold Rush called "Bering Sea Gold". Adding further insult by adding salt to the wound was that the new show immediately followed after Gold Rush.

Recognizing competition within "his" Gold Rush, Todd split his group into competing rivals using different methods of mining: one with Todd, Jack and Jim and the other with Greg, Dave and Chris. When the latter group was pulling away quickly and Todd capitulated back into one group again, he capped a record mining season but fell short of a targeted one thousand ounce goal.

In order to rejuvenate a slip in ratings, Todd's fourth season takes an enormous, deliberately leap for ONE season. No matter how successful or unsuccessful they were to be in South America, Todd conspires with Discovery Channel to make it a one shot deal. This was done in order to jump start a new personal journey for season five (back in the Yukon). Season four in Guyana was simply a break in the action, a diversion from the other rivals in the Yukon and more importantly, an excuse to make season five look like a new trek of redemption.

Todd needed to hit not only a home run in season eight, but a grand slam. He has got to pull the biggest rabbit out of his hat to date. Otherwise, it's time to throw in the towel and hit the showers.

No matter what happens, let's keep everything in proper perspective - that it's only a television serial with a lot of money and jobs riding on it. It was a means to an end, especially for Todd, and each must answer to a higher authority

MY 2 CENTS

(or Discovery Channel's Lowest Low in Getting Ratings)

You can bamboozle your way to achieve any means to an end through trickery, intimation, hoodwink or deception. But when the need to attain the highest ratings--> sponsors--> money, you compromise integrity, and you have to draw the line.

James tells me that:

> "Friends, relatives, fans and complete strangers call or stop me asking why I resorted to stealing in the show."

Not watching any of the episodes on live television, I had no idea what they were talking about until I saw it for myself on someone's replay (VHS recorder). Even to his last days he said, "I'll never forgive them for using and smearing me that way!"

Harness was being accused ("shown") on Discovery for stealing gold in the promo for the following week's episode. Even though there was nothing on the show itself that related to the promo of James in the following new episode on Friday, the damage to his reputation was already done.

I don't know why "reality TV" has to resort to this. Many loyal Gold Rush viewers (as well as myself) feel that an apology was in order at that time, if not for the sake of the late James Harness, then at least for his family who have to bear his name and legacy.

2014 CHRISTMAS+1

While passing through the Northwest, I stopped by Sandy the morning after Christmas to drop off some green tea confections to my friends. I forgot where Chris lived so I went driving like a headless chicken street by street until I stopped in front of a driveway. I didn't want to call that early in the morning and wake them up. I looked through the driver's side window of a F350 and recognized those work gloves we wore up in the Yukon. I hung two tied clear bags of green tea cookies (his wife's favorite is green tea powder, not green tea leaves) and went to Greg's place.

I didn't recognize the small house at first so I went further down the road and returned. Still smelling the smoke of an abandoned house that was more than half burnt to the ground (I was told that Greg purposely did it the night before), I walked through a new gated metal fence that bordered the frontage. I dropped off a couple of bags of green tea cookies for his family on the door handle of a new home and left a phone greeting on Greg's cellphone.

I next went to the airport across the street but decided not to enter since the code numbers for the locked gate had changed. When I returned to Chris' home and saw the items on the door latch missing, I was going to leave him with more cookies. All of a sudden, Chris tore open the door and surprised (scared) me. Chris bear hugged me and invited me inside for a very nice time of catch-up conversation and fellowship.

I thanked both of them for their role in coordinating my message regarding the passing of James Harness last summer. I needed to notify Todd and his group of James' passing. Chris was unreachable via his and others' cell phones so I called his wife. She had the means to contact him. They email each other almost daily to keep in close communication. I told her that it was a very important message that needed to be conveyed. It required immediate attention but it was not a life and death situation. Planning for attendance to a funeral required them to be excused from the shoot, a transport to the airport and a flight back home on more than one plane. When Chris returned my phone call the very next day, I broke the sad news of James' passing and asked him to inform Greg and somehow find a way to inform Todd and the rest of the group.

Chris told me that Greg took the news very hard. While at Chris' Sandy home, I mentioned that I recently rendezvoused with Greg in Palm Springs to personally convey James' last words. Greg told me that upon learning of James passing, he immediately stopped working. Since no particular film crew participated in the shooting of every season of Gold Rush (most did not even film beyond Parker's entourage), Greg invited whatever crew members of RAW that were present to tell them who James Harness was and the role he played in making Gold Rush such a success (Discovery later played the filming of Greg's message). Greg then asked me whether James accepted Christ as his Savior. I said only God knows and we cannot and should not render judgment. I can tell Greg was deeply moved and most concerned with James' eternity.

Weeks before I accompanied Todd's convoy on the Alaskan and Yukon Gold Rush trek, I recounted to Greg the moments of simple talk to hours of lengthy discussions that James and I had about eschatology, origins, history, Scripture, and what not. Let it be known now that I am not paying my respects to James here, i.e., making his image or memory bigger or better than it really was. I worked with him throughout the time we spent together. We shared our intellect when standing down and socialized after work over a gourmet meal he cooked or when eating out. This is the primary reason why I was so fortunate to have James so involved in working with me after he left Gold Rush. If you don't know already, you certainly don't have to graduate from Stanford or Harvard's MBA program to be smart. Returning to Greg's (and everyone else's) concern, I believe that we can rest assured of what James did – that we should place our trust in Him for eternal life and definitely not in ourselves.

I was happy to mention to Chris that my highlight of 2014 was simply reading the Scriptures from the beginning to the end in one year. The same was done by our Founding Fathers more than 200 years ago, as I recently learned from history in D.C. For example, both Presidents Jefferson and Adams read the Bible cover to cover each year for many years. I learned that when you read the Scriptures, read it like you are sitting at the very feet of God and He is speaking to you directly. Chris took a good, deep sigh in hearing this.

Almost the entire gamut of past, present and future was brought out in the precious few minutes we had: plans and strategies for our professional careers and counterparts on Gold Rush. You can write an entire book from this alone. Here's a small tidbit – regarding my plans to produce television shows, I didn't like the idea of a show that was proposed by Chris; it centered on farming. Even though farming represented the backbone of our country, longstanding myths may be difficult to overcome. Chris then asks me of what I thought of a charitable, non-profit like Wounded Warriors. He wanted to give himself (time and money) to this fine organization. Although I served on the board of directors in many charities and non-profit organizations throughout my life in which I never wanted monetary compensation, I had no personal knowledge of Wounded Warriors' financial books or records. [Check, for example, with Charity Watch and other watchdog agencies, including the BBB and your State AG-Attorney General-as well as the IRS in evaluating its 501(c)(3) non-profit status in order to determine if that organization is using your gifts for the intended need it purports to represent and not significantly for their overhead or anyone's personal expenses]. I said that Wounded Warriors was undoubtedly a most worthy organization that provided recreational therapy for great men and women serving our country. But before sending your hard-earned money to anyone, especially The Wounded Warrior Foundation, first perform at least some level of due diligence. Chris said that he proposed the Wounded Warrior concept to RAW and/or Discovery but it was rejected for showing "handicapped" people where TV audiences may get squeamish or uncomfortable over. I said "wait". That was one of the 100 shows that I wrote a treatment about that one night at the Sandy Airport lodge before we left for Alaska. He agrees but said the approach would be different since it would require actors to portray the original injury that befell the actual person. Reality then sets in when they make a recovery (physically and mentally) and they take on the world again. I agree.

  I did want to thank Chris also for getting the word out to Greg, Todd, Jack and others when I informed him of James' passing after I left James' Redmond home. It was hoped that they may want to start making plans to attend the funeral service.

  James had told me that he was tearfully touched and humbled, and appreciated the support of Todd, et al., for his mother after he decided to stay and work with Todd during the first season as she was dying. James kind of apologized to me for crying but I said that here's nothing wrong with a grown man acting that way when you consider that Jesus wept too. He regained his composure and smiled as he climbed into his truck and took me out to eat at his friend's restaurant (one of Kato's best meals ever).

  We fondly talked a little bit more about James but Sharon interjected the same sentiment with Chris that,

    "James was not a good worker."

  In my mind I chose not to take exception to their statement and changed topics quickly.

  At that very instance, too, I decided to set the record straight by parole evidence, to write the real story of Gold Rush and end a lot of spurious speculation that had come about since season one.

After recounting with this thought, I finished the great cup of black coffee (I only drink about 4 to 5 cups of coffee a year), thanked Sharon, got a hearty handshake followed by another bear hug (maybe Chris should try out for the WWE) and back slapping, I then said goodbye to Chris. THIS became my defining moment as to why I am writing this book; to set the record straight.

EPILOGUE

It is now known that James had really serious medical issues that resulted from being rear-ended in an accident years ago. Post operative treatments were temporal and, at best, addressed the symptoms and not the cause of his medical injuries. Like Chris, I wanted James to have the best medical attention. Stanford Medical Center was a no-brainer. Suggestion was made for addressing his lingering back vertebrae issue but James wanted to wait until he resolved his tax problem(s). He did not want, nor had he ever requested external funding from me, just compensation for employment as an astute consultant once we get the ball rolling. Topics of discussion leading to fruition include filming in Australia, Asia and elsewhere. Pending his health, James would use his contacts already in place there and execute plans and strategies with relative ease. I choose to not disclose any proposed or pending projects on the burner. Besides James, we have consultants from coast to coast assisting, advising and, most importantly, critiquing areas of concern. What I miss most about James is not only his many areas of expertise but his ability to think through a concept and manifest it into practical reality. It literally has taken several individuals to "replace" all the areas of his expertise. Like in all life, try to do the best you can and just reminisce back to find inspiration to go on and succeed.

Without leaving James' legacy unfulfilled, I intend to carry on with as many of the projects we planned. I just hope that James won't mind that at least I am going to try to meet his exacting expectations the best way possible.

After "Gold Rush", what's next? Borrowing Al Jolson's line from the "The Jazz Singer", "You ain't seen nothing yet."

Addendum

Bloomberg Business just reported in the week of August 17, 2015, that gold mining companies are scaling back the number of employees by a third to compensate the nearly 40% drop in the price of gold since 2011, thereby ensuring continued operations in a diminishing valued commodity. One week before this report, cable and network television have seen a significant drop in the value of their companies as well as their broadcast acquisitions recently made during that same period. Combined, these two factors do not bode well for major network broadcasters relying on programming with less viewership appeal.

DOUBT ME? AUTHOR'S NOTES

This is a work of nonfiction. As a "whistleblower", you now realize the intensity that Discovery constantly used in its attempts to require me to sign confidentiality and nondisclosure statements. With substantial money from corporate sponsors (advertising and commercial revenue based on continued, declining ratings) and syndication literally on the line, they will now try to find every reason to discredit me. "Can you doubt my veracity and observations?"

Please ask Todd, Jack, Chris, Jim, Dave or Greg if I have given false testimony to any of the foregoing events, testimony and observations that were objectively made. I have qualified my remarks that were made subjectively and in all fairness. There is no consideration requested or demanded by me for any of the statements made. The events and experiences detailed herein are all true and have been faithfully rendered as I have remembered and recorded them, to the best of my ability. Prefaced comments were stated to the best of my recollection with parole evidence backing it. Conversations come from my keen recollection of them: those with word-for-word documentation are in quotation marks. All photos are accurate and none were edited. To date, no consideration was ever offered for my assistance in serving at the pleasure of the Hoffmans with the exception of friendship, which is priceless. I thank each member of Todd's crew for their undying faith and the friendship that they have extended to me as a brother in arms then (and now).

It has been stated that Gold Rush was filmed entirely as reality TV and recorded as a Muscidae (housefly) on the wall saw it. After James left Gold Rush, he said

> "I couldn't talk about many details of the show due to confidentiality clauses in my contract. Now no longer with the show, the sky's the limit."

"I don't care if it's falling down or killing yourself, they want to see it again and get 2 shots of it."

"It's really hard to have a competitive business and put everything into that - trying to make a profit you built out of the ground – and yet to do a TV show at the same time. They collide constantly. It slows you down so much, there's no way to succeed. You're doing two different things at the same time."

RAW's filming "were pushy about what they wanted to get, even if it was not what you would have done in a normal day."

"For every 40 hours of filming, you might see 2 minutes of it. And sometimes it's what you leave out that's important."

As Kato would say, "I'm the messenger, not the message."

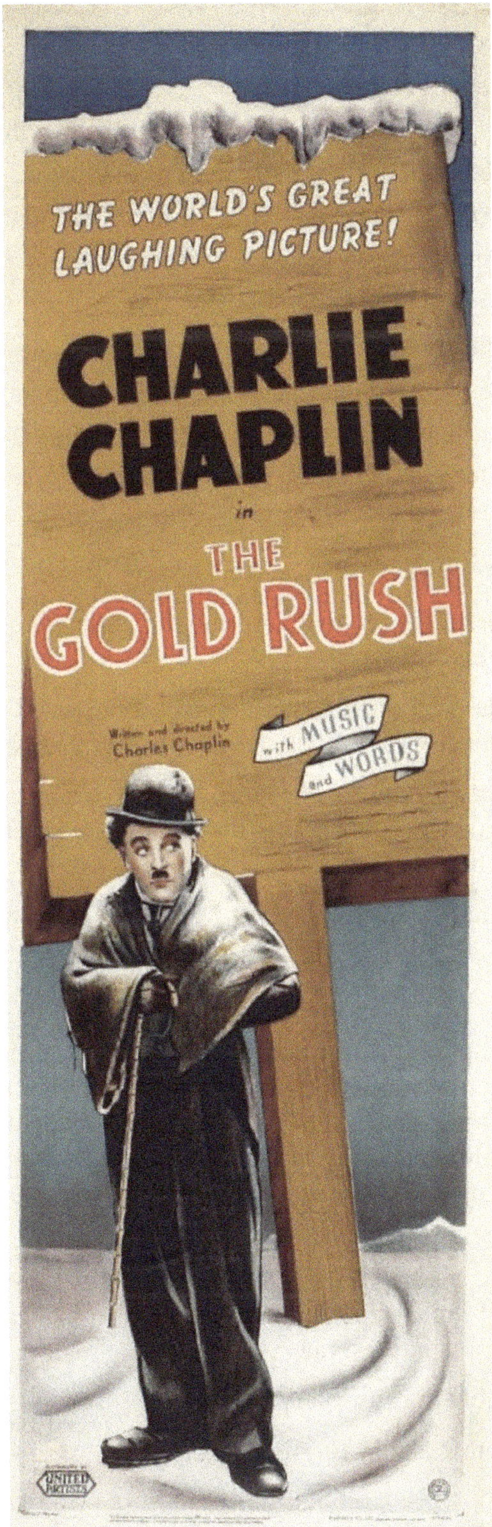
THE WORLD'S GREAT LAUGHING PICTURE!
CHARLIE CHAPLIN
in
THE GOLD RUSH
Written and directed by Charles Chaplin
with MUSIC and WORDS
UNITED ARTISTS

GLOSSARY

BDU = battle dress uniform

CMH = Congressional Medal of Honor

Carpe diem = seize the day; enjoy the present, as opposed to placing all hope in the future

Corollary = an immediate consequence or early drawn conclusion

Eschatology = any system of doctrines concerning last, or final matters, as death or the afterlife

Estoppel = a bar or impediment preventing a party from asserting a fact or a claim inconsistent with a position he previously took

GWOT=Global War On Terrorism

Hermeneutics = the science of interpretation, to make clear, explanatory

Logistics = the branch of military science and operations dealing with the procurement, supply, and maintenance of equipment, the movement of personnel, the provision of facilities, and with related matters

French logistique = quartermaster's work

Muscidae = belonging or pertaining to the family of dipterous (two-winged) insects that includes the common housefly

Myopia = a condition of the eye in which parallel rays are focused in front of the retina, objects being seen distinctly only when near to the eye; nearsightedness

Parole evidence = a rule that oral evidence cannot be used to contradict the terms of a written contract or such matters; by reducing oral discussions, redirects, rights and duties to writing in accordance between parties

Perma frost = perennially frozen subsoil

Provost marshal = Army, an officer on the staff of a commander, charged with police functions

Res ipsa locquitor = the things speaks for itself; a rule of law or evidence whereby the negligence of an alleged wrongdoer can be inferred from the fact that the accident happened; inference or presumption of negligence arising upon proof that the instrumentality or condition causing the injury was in the exclusive control of the defendant and the accident was one that ordinarily does not occur in the absence of negligence

Rule of 72 = actuarial mathematical function to derive an approximation for money to double – 72 divided by the __% rate = the approximate number of years it takes to double your money at the given simple interest rate

Soporific = causing or tending to cause sleep

Toynbee, Arnold = Twentieth-Century English historian

PHOTO GALLERY

Hall of Famer John Madden

38th President

39ᵗʰ President

41ˢᵗ President

208

42nd President

Senator John McCain

The late Senator Fred Thompson

Burt Reynolds

Isabella Rossellini

Tom Arnold

Bernadette Peters on Broadway

At The Tonight Show

Jay Leno

Paul Shaffer after the The Late Show

Mr. & Mrs. Carl Karcher

Senator Barbara Boxer

Senator Diane Feinstein

Lunch break at the Fisher's

A camera crew in Dawson City

Off the tortuous Yukon Road

U.S. – Canadian border

Summer family dinner on Father's Day 2011

Airport-lodge auditorium

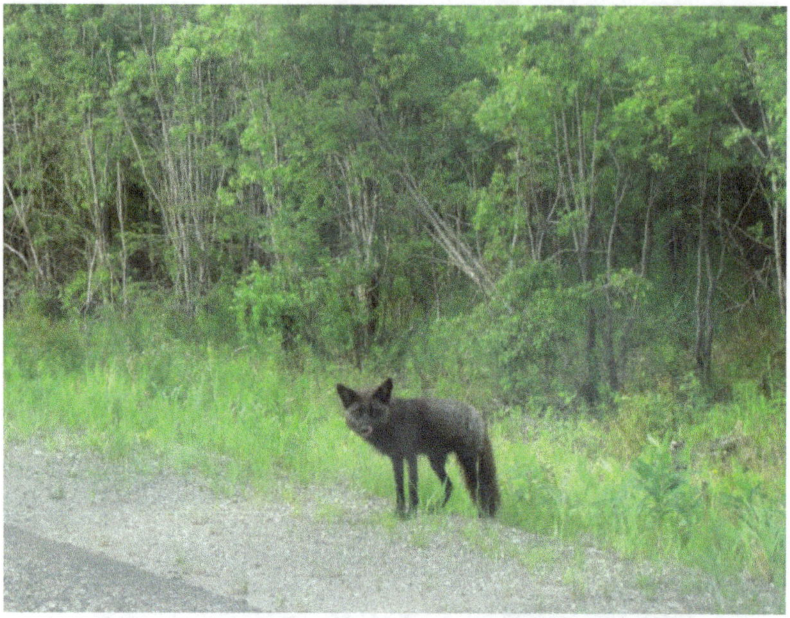

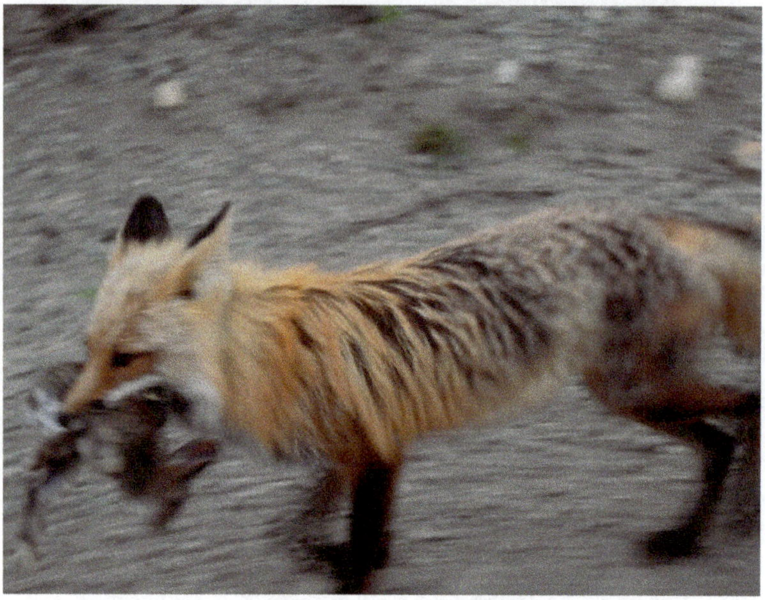

Todd's youngest son offers Cheetos

Kato offers one

River crossing

Really that close!

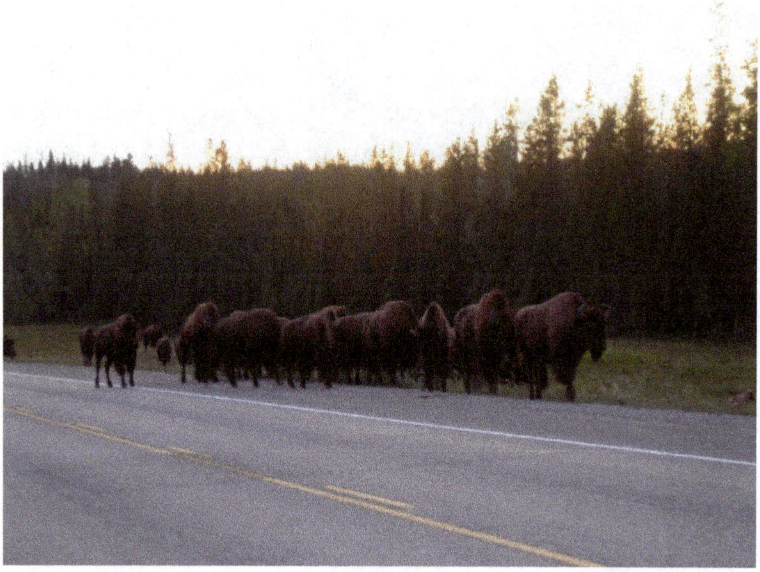

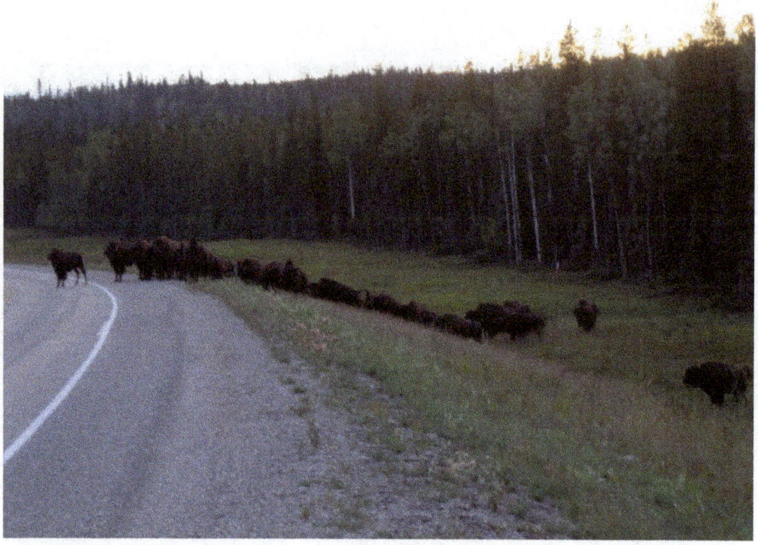

Checking out real estate properties for the Gold Rush team a few blocks away from the Dawson City RV park

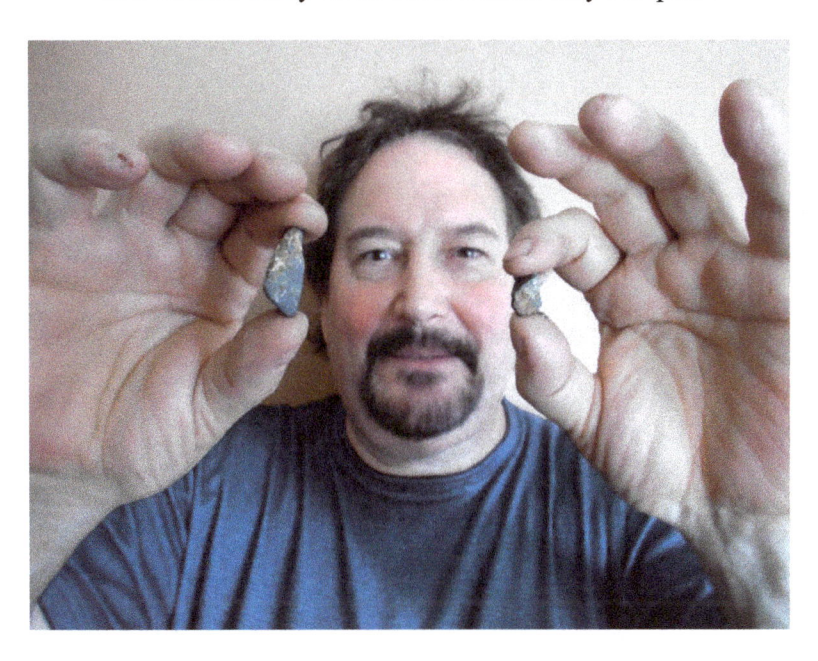

All GOLD RUSH book sale proceeds shall be donated to families of fallen soldiers from 09-11 GWOT.